TALES OF A MYSTIC PSYCHIC

KATHLEEN DUQUETTE

TALES OF A MYSTIC PSYCHIC

ISBN-10: 0979868882
ISBN-13: 978-0979868887

Publisher:
1st House Publishing
Attn: Martha Theus
8939 S. Sepulveda Blvd., Suite 110-1024
Los Angeles, CA 90045 U.S.A.
(424) 249-9355
MarthaTheus@gmail.com

Any resemblance to the living or dead is purely supernatural…

CONTENTS

OM MANI PADME HUM

Chapter 1

First Reading with Liz

I remember Liz sitting in front of me in the client reading chair in my small, perfectly square reading room. (Oh, how I loved that little reading room. Oh, how I loved it being a perfect square.) I recall Liz's eyes – beautiful, agitated, full of expression. On that day, Liz's two primary concerns were her marriage to Topher and her dear friend, Renata.

Here's what I received on Liz and Topher's past life: Medici family, heavy velvet fur-trimmed gowns, ornate jewelry. She sponsored him in "artistic" ventures. Translation: Topher was Liz's gigolo. They ritualistically initiated each other into the decadent life, taking each other to newer and lower lows. Long orgiastic days. Lavish banqueting. Alcohol ... drugs ... As reincarnation goes, Liz and Topher found each other in this life and immediately fell into their obsession again.

We moved on to Liz's closest friend, Renata. She and Renata had been twins in another life. Atlantis? Renata was the leader in the friendship.

1

Liz was far from done with Topher and was very fragile in her need for Renata's support. It all felt so unfinished, but it was as far as I could go that day.

Almost three years would pass before I would see Liz again.

OM MANI PADME HUM

Chapter 2

Fast Forward: Liz's Second Reading

May 1988, Liz returned and sat in front of me, once again – pale, fragile, shaky. Humbled and broken, she asked for help with her drinking. I could feel the spirit within me quivering; it was now or never, this moment wasn't going to come again. I had to take a risk. I had to tell the truth. Feeling dread and anxiety, I gently told Liz, "You're an alcoholic." I asked if she was ready to do something about it and she said, "Yes." I told her my husband, Marc DuQuette, was a Recovery Counselor and happened to be home. Did she want to meet him? Again, she said, "Yes." Liz later told me that the walk from my little reading room, across our small home, over to Marc was one of the longest walks of her life. Liz's Destiny was about to change.

The following Saturday, Liz was scheduled to come in to see Marc for a session. Her husband, Topher, insisted on bringing her. On the way down, he pulled over and parked in a nearby neighborhood. He yanked Liz by the hair into the back of the van, where no one could see them, and beat her. It was a miracle she made it to her session with Marc that day.

Over the next few years, Marc and Liz did intensive recovery work and by the grace of God,"One Day at a Time," Liz has been blessed with the miracle of sobriety for over 25 years.

The entire process of divorcing Topher took Liz two and half years - a "jaws of life" karmic de-mangling. The negative power did not want Liz to get out of that marriage. The power of her sobriety was an exorcism.

One last, disturbing note.   Although I never met Topher on the physical plane, late one night in a cell-like void, I had an encounter with Topher in the astral. He looked ghoulish, dead. I knew he was about to attack me and I jerked back into my physical body.

As we psychics say: "Confirmation."

Chapter 3

The Baba Sisters

Many years ago I had a client come to me. She was a good client and I saw her for several sessions. She referred me to her friends from up the coast. A group of three women flew down to see me. I can still remember the intense energy of their sessions. One of the three women, Sandy, invited me to her home to do a reading tour. Thus began my great adventure of many years, going up the coast to do readings at Sandra and Christopher's home.

Sandy's associate, royal Leo, Karen, played a major part in my sessions. Karen had great respect for my work and went out of her way to contact clients for me when I came up to work.

Sandy and Karen were Baba Sisters, followers of the great Indian Avatar, Sathya Sai Baba*. They traveled to India as often as possible to see their beloved Swami. Sandy and Karen's devotion to Sai Baba was very sweet. Sandy, in particular (Aries), had a childlike heart connection to Swami. On many of their trips to Sai Baba's ashram, they were blessed with the great privilege of receiving a private audience with the great Avatar.

Swirling his hands outside of time and space in the Etheric Realm, Sai Baba manifested sacred gifts for Sandy and Karen. I well remember the beautiful Navratan ring Baba materialized for Sandy. The Navratan represents the nine planets. To wear this ring is to wear protection from the vibrational forces of the planets.

The long drive up the coast completed. Nervous anticipation as the car advanced past the horses, up the steep curving driveway bordered by beautiful towering pine trees. Finally crossing the threshold of Sandy and Chris' home, entering *another world*.

Sandy and Chris had a large home which they had remodeled themselves over the years. They were in the publishing business and they once told me that with every book they published they would renovate another room in the house.

Their home was phenomenal! It had a large, elegant backyard with a pool surrounded by flagstones. They were very fond of flowers. Chris not only did the landscaping, he also did all the yard work. I remember sitting in their screened-in sunroom, looking out at the beautiful, tranquil garden (as I was often too busy with my work to spend time outside) marveling at Chris' intuitive flair with the plant kingdom.

When Sandy's mother passed away, they filled their home with her antiques. In the main hall of the house hanging upon the glossy, adobe-like off-white walls were large, beautiful, mandala oil paintings of the chakras. Sandy collected Tibetan Thankas and artifacts from around the world. Sandy sponsored a Northern California artist, Royce, who did lush marble sculptures. There were stained glass windows throughout the house, and of course, many beautiful pictures of Sai Baba, including a small grouping of Baba, framed in silver filigree... exquisite!

When I was in Sandy and Chris' home I constantly sensed Sai Baba's potent presence. One night I had a dream that a python was swimming through the house. Swami. I deeply enjoyed reading Sandy's books written by Sathya Sai Baba devotees. My heart chakra would expand as I reflected upon how the true core of all paths is Love.

Their home had a spiritual, yet opulent, energy. I loved this energy and I loved doing readings at the Baba house. If I were to describe the overall energy I felt coming through while I did readings there, it would be like everything was always peaking . . . a cresting wave that never broke. The power never really came back down again properly. It was high energy but hard to navigate up there. It's a big deal having psychic readings in your home. It can be very disruptive. Every day the energy becoming stronger, and stronger, and stronger only coming down when I finally get into my "Gipsy caravan" and leave.

Chris, a very conservative Libran with the Moon in Capricorn, was, I sensed, in part fascinated and perhaps equally perplexed by all the spiritual, psychic happenings Sandy scheduled in their home. We all agreed that the best time for me to come up and do sessions was when Chris was off on business. All female ~ Moon Magic ~ Goddess Time. The appointments set up much more easily. Everything flowed.

Sandy and Karen had an Indian friend, Geeta, who lived in the United Kingdom. Geeta was a professional psychic with quite a following. She had even been featured on the BBC. Often when I would contact Sandy about coming up to the house to do sessions, Geeta would call a few days later wanting the same time slot. Geeta and I . . . such a complex karma. I used to muse: "Geeta, an Indian psychic living in Ireland and me, an Irish psychic who travels to India". To add to the mystery, we both have the same Spiritual Teacher and there aren't that many of us throughout the world.

So, for several years, Sandy and Karen had been telling me about Geeta, whom I had yet to meet. I felt like I knew her, just not on the Earth plane. Finally, during one of my trips to do sessions at Sandy and Chris' I did meet Geeta.

Geeta was a very powerful Capricorn. She was rather short, wearing a silk, saffron-coloured, sadhu-like, salwar kameeze which exuded a pungent Indian oil. Paradoxically, Geeta radiated a terribly shy, fierce energy. A feverish fire blazed in her brilliant, dark, Indian eyes.

Sandy and Karen urged me to exchange readings with Geeta. Because they were my esteemed hosts, I just let go and agreed. However, quite honestly I had to admit there was a sense of Destiny: the two of us finally meeting … it was futile to resist … this was my Fate.

As Geeta and I set up our sessions (she was going to read me first), she said, "Something that happened to you in 1977 is about to happen again!" I felt fear and anxiety course through my body. I don't operate much in Time. Yet, back in the Seventies, I had had so many difficult, painful experiences I sunk, desperately trying to remember what the hell had happened to me in 1977! With an icky, sick feeling, I called my husband, Marc, to quell my panic. Marc listened very carefully and I received his sage counsel. Marc implied it was an old Gypsy trick intended scare me and throw me off-balance. I was now grounded and ready for my reading with Geeta.

Sure enough, when Geeta did read me, it was excruciating. Geeta began my reading with a high-pitched scream. So shocking and bizarre I almost jumped out of my chair! Geeta told me she was channeling sounds that she had "received" to clear negative energy. Anyway, thanks to Marc's help, I'd made my mind up I was going to "hold my mud" and take her reading like a man. And, I did.

When it was my turn to read Geeta, I felt great wells of love and compassion envelope us. Our Spiritual Teacher, clearly with us. Grace.

The tale I've just told you is only one of my many unusual psychic experiences at the Baba house over the years.

Sandy, Chris, their daughters, Tarah, Carter, and Sandy's associate, Karen were all very supportive of me as a psychic. I was cared-for and welcomed. They all honored and respected the healing energy of the sessions.

I had a karmic connection to Tarah and Carter preparing for their eventual marriages. After the girls got married, my destiny with this loving group of people started to fade. It felt as if my karma had been fulfilled. My work, for now, was done.

The Baba Sisters taught me to become confident and sure of myself doing reading tours. My time with them built up the powerful psychic muscles I needed to channelize the extreme energy that a good reading tour demands. In this respect, Sandy and Karen were my living spirit guides, helping me achieve the monumental task of bearing the crushing vortex of the reading tours. Remember, as I said earlier, a good reading tour is like a tidal wave. You have to be in the electrical force field of the daily readings to "get" how incredibly intense it is riding that wave. A reading tour is an all-consuming experience. The Baba Sisters honored this intensity and said, "Bring it on!" They gave me the courage to plunge deeper and deeper into the ocean of knowledge and intuition readings require. Their faith, support, and friendship shaped me forever to evolve into the Intuitive Counselor that I am today. In eternal gratitude I pranam you, Baba Sisters!

*On Easter Sunday, April 24th, 2011, Sathya Sai Baba shed his mortal coil, merging back into God.

How you climb up the mountain is just as important as how you get down the mountain. And so it is with life, which for many of us becomes one big gigantic test, followed by one big gigantic lesson. In the end, it all comes down to one word. Grace. It's how you accept winning and losing, good luck and bad luck, the darkness and the light.

Philosophy®

Chapter 4

Ill-Fated Couple

n attractive woman who was clearly very much on edge came to see me one day. She quickly laid out a deeply disturbing scenario.

Her husband's grandfather had killed his wife. Unbelievably, my client's grandmother had killed her husband. I told her, "Leave your husband now! He thinks it's *his* destiny to kill you!" My client did not seem surprised. We stared at each other. We both knew the truth.

I never saw her again.

Chapter 5

Coco

My wealthy, ostentatious, Jewish client, Coco, dressed bizarrely. Think of Cher doing a comedy skit, except this was Coco's real look. I loved Coco's big, chunky rings and odd fashion sense.

Coco's husband had left her for a younger woman, but he wouldn't let Coco go. Although Coco was divorced, she had a secret affair with a man she felt was beneath her. This man "got" Coco. He loved her.

I remember our last session, regarding her affair. Time went so slow. I felt sweaty, uncomfortable. The words were dragged out of me, "If you don't really let him into your life, he'll be taken from you." He died shortly thereafter.

About four years later, Coco died in a plane crash. I'm sure her ex never recovered.

Ideally, couples need three lives.

One for him, one for her, and one for them together.

Jacqueline Bisset

Chapter 6

Lambs to the Slaughter

On our way back from India, Shanti and Skipper and I were visiting friends in Ireland. It was 7am and I was wondering why Shanti and Skipper weren't up yet. They were scheduled to see Lee Ann, a local Irish psychic at 9am. So, I went into their bedroom to check on them. They were still in bed with their blankets pulled up to their chins, their eyes like saucers. It was crystal clear they did not want to go to their readings. They were scared. Being a psychic myself, I knew Shanti and Skipper were "tuning in". Something was afoot. Something was terribly wrong. They reluctantly got ready to go and I went with them to check this woman out.

Lee Ann opened her door and I was standing there.

Staring deep into her eyes, I mentally warned her: "Don't hurt these girls!" I turned around and left, and Shanti and Skipper went in for their sessions.

Two hours later, Shanti and Skipper staggered out the door in a blackout. They could hardly walk. I was silently hysterical looking at them. I begged them to tell me every detail of their experience. They told me Lee Ann had used a large deck of playing cards with solid black backs. They described to me her white, white hands, her long, long fingernails - also black - as she laid out all the cards in the deck. I thought, "Uh-oh! She used all the cards! Not good!" They told me that after I left, Lee Ann sharply turned to them, and said, "Who was that? She gave me the bo-huh!"

Lee Ann called out Skipper's husband's name several times during Shanti's reading. Skipper could hear everything; she was only eight feet away in the same room. Shanti later told me privately that Skipper's head jerked up when she heard her husband's name. And, although we were laughing hysterically as they shared their readings with me, Skipper later acted suspicious of Shanti.

During this trip to Ireland, we often went to a wonderful vegetarian restaurant that featured readers. The Escape* was owned by a cool, 1942 Gemini, sailor-type, named Tom. This guy had a lot of style. A proud monarch holding court, I can still remember Tom sitting there in his navy blue peacoat, rolling his own cigarettes. Tom filled his restaurant with art collected from around the world. The Escape was really well-named. Every time we went there, I felt time slip away. I loved sitting in The Escape, looking out at the stormy Irish Sea.

Shanti wanted to be cleansed of her horrible experience with Lee Ann, so she scheduled a Tarot reading at The Escape. Kevin, who read her cards, gave Shanti a very thoughtful, caring reading, full of healing energy. And, it came true!

* Sorry folks, The Escape closed many years ago.

Chapter 7

The Arsenal

aughter and separated husband. Wild country people. In the session, I saw guns and knives everywhere. The mother, my client, confirmed that her son-in-law had a huge arsenal and always threatened to kill her daughter.

I never saw or heard from the mother again.

Chapter 8

A Mother in Distress

My client asked about her son, a professional in the Pacific Northwest. Although her son was doing great, he was seeing prostitutes and she was very concerned. I told her there's nothing stronger than the psychic bond between a mother and child. I told her to psychically "send" to him to stop frequenting the prostitutes. Two weeks later he completely stopped.

She never told him about her psychic intervention.

Don't stop working. Just stop worrying.

T-Bone Burnett

Chapter 9

Sanskara

J went to the Renaissance Faire. I saw a somber, elderly yogi in silk saffron robes. He had long beautiful wavy gray hair, a lined noble face, hooded piercing eyes. He gave me a remarkable palm reading. He uttered one sentence: "Your Destiny is meditation." I sat with him for the rest of the day. Although we were at the Renaissance Faire for hours, there was no time. We were in another region. He looked like Paramahansa Yogananda did right before he died and ~ yes! ~ he was Yogananda, who drew me back to himself to complete our karma.

Chapter 10

The United Church of Revelations

Spiritualism
ESP, clairvoyance, extrasensory perception, insight,
mind-reading,parapsychology,premonition,presentiment,
second sight,sixth sense,telepathic transmission,
telesthesia,thought transference.

How do I even begin to describe my oceanic experience at the United Church of Revelations? I don't remember how long Revelations lasted or when it disbanded but when I was there, there was a lot going on. It was happening! Here is how Revelations was for me in its heyday:

The United Church of Revelations, formerly a mortuary that Reverend Richard Vallandingham, AKA Reverend Dick, converted into a spiritualist church. Down in the area where the bodies had been embalmed was where we held our classes. There were no windows and (needless to say) the ceiling was pretty low.

I remember during the mortuary renovation, one of Reverend Dick's volunteers ~ semi-homeless, rageaholic Gypsy Tom ~ ranting and raving about cleaning the blood off the floor, walls, and ceiling in the bloodletting room. As memory serves, I believe our classes were held in that former bloodletting room.

About eight or so dramatically oversized ghoulish spirit guide pictures lined the walls down there in our classroom. I can recall one of those pictures: a large pastel rendering of a stately Fu Manchu-ish Oriental lord containing lots of sickly shades of green. Windowless, even when the lights were on the room felt dark ... cold. Quite a place to hold Psychic Development classes!

Reverend Dick lived in the upstairs apartment where the funeral home director used to stay. The United Church of Revelations' services were held at night in a small chapel contained on the mortuary property.

Reverend Dick considered the Apostle Paul to be his personal spirit guide. (He said so.)

Those rowdy, turbulent classes! To this day, I don't know exactly what I learned during my studies at Revelations, but I did do scores of practice readings. It was read, read, read, read, read!

Everyone in our classes was romantically crossed. Everyone had a *thing* about somebody who had a *thing* about somebody else. Because of all the crossed romantic energy, there were occasional freak-outs among the less mentally stable members of Revelations. Intense!

Reverend Dick used to play New Age music during his Guided Meditations. When he was done he would say, "Shield your eyes! Cover your eyes! I'm about to turn the lights on!"

Whenever Reverend Dick would start a comment with "I say this with love," we knew we were in big trouble. "I say this with love" from Reverend Dick was a comment to be avoided at all costs. Translation: beaming his Plutonian laser gaze, psychically tapping his Scorpion stinger, channelizing the God-awful "I say this with love," one of us was about to have our character defects revealed and dissected in a group setting.

My friend, Avonlee, used to receive counseling and healing treatments from Reverend Dick. To my great consternation, Avonlee called Reverend Dick "Father Dick." Exasperated I used to say, "Why don't you call him Reverend Dick like the rest of us, Avonlee?"

Charismatic Scorpio, vulnerable Moon in Cancer ~ women were crazy about Reverend Dick while some of the men in the congregation were quite competitive towards him. As far as I could tell, Reverend Dick always won. He lived in a mesmerizing, psychic realm of his own.

After the Psychic Development classes, we used to go to Denny's ... a bunch of us in a booth ... blissfully chain smoking, drinking coffee, giving each other (what else?) psychic impressions until 2:00 or 3:00am. Among the seven or eight of us in the booth, we might order two English muffins. Cheap. Needless to say, the repetitive impressions started to get very, very stale. One *can* read a subject to death.

Like the soap opera "All My Children's" Pine Valley Ball where the multiple marriages, remarriages, impending divorces met for a night, such were our "Old Home Week" church services at Revelations. Emotions ran high. A raging fever. Old, old karmic contacts fraught with tremendous tension, feeling, attraction, pain. A Full Moon out of control. Remember ... everyone had a *thing* about somebody who had a *thing* about somebody else.

Once, Reverend Dick was going to be meeting some of the United Revelations church ladies at Denny's. He was very nervous about walking in alone ~ their own personal Tom Jones. The waves of female longing bombarding him from the booths. (I could almost hear "What's New Pussycat?" floating through the restaurant!) So,

Reverend Dick asked me to walk through Denny's with him. My pleasure! I was very protective of my old friend. Exuding great confidence and style, we strolled in together pretending to be deeply engrossed in a private conversation.

Reverend Dick was a cross between Robert Duvall ("The Apostle,") Frank Sinatra ("My Way,") with a splash of Richard Dawson's cool Scorpio energy thrown in. An Old School spiritualist, claiming Divine Inspiration. Yet, in another sense, Reverend Dick was a classy Vegas entertainer, working the lounge.

One night, in the chapel at Revelations during one of Reverend Dick's spiritualist services, Reverend Dick announced that I would be giving spot readings after the service. Reverend Dick had given me absolutely no warning that he was going to volunteer my psychic abilities that evening. But, of course, I couldn't let my friend down. Later, as I went down the line doing my mini-readings, I tuned into a woman who said she, too, was a psychic. She took over and gave me an impression. She received that I would meet my soul mate in this life . . . that her clients always wanted this special impression, but she could hardly ever give it . . .

Please indulge me, Dear Reader, as I must wind up these tales of my time with Reverend Dick at the United Church of Revelations. My memories there are endless...

The United Church of Revelations was my training ground...

my stomping ground...

myburningoutaddictivelyobsessivelycompulsivelyreadingground...

my womb...my birth into my life as a psychic.

Where would I be today without you, Reverend Dick?

Chapter 11

What's Going to Happen Has Already Happened

im and I met when we were kids in high school. Kim was a double Sagittarius with Aries Moon. Intellectually brilliant, Kim was also a classic beauty: blonde blonde hair, blue blue eyes, tall, slim, lanky. We were both consumed by the occult, paranormal, psychic worlds. When we were together, weird, astonishing things would happen!

After high school, when Kim was on break between colleges, we shared an apartment on Cinnabar Street. While waiting for Kim to come home, I could psychically hear her Sagittarian Jupiter Footsteps blocks away. Boom, boom, boom ~ crashed in my Inner Ear.

Time passed and I was slipping. The realm between the physical and astral was becoming very blurry. Not grounded, I was nearly out of the body almost all the time.

Feeling apprehensive one evening, I told Kim I needed to go rest. I went into the other room and lay down. Instantly I left the body. I was out in the astral, pushed through a portal into a past life. There, I was a Medieval healer dwelling alone in a thatched hut in the forest. Kim was a noblewoman who would steal away from her husband to bring me food and supplies. Superstitiously regarded as a witch, people who judged and condemned me by day came to me secretly by night for healing and psychic guidance.

On this moonless night, I divined that a villainous group of men were riding to my hut to take my life. I recognized all of these men from my present incarnation. I knew every one of them. As the Masters in India say, "What's going to happen has already happened." Straining, unable to get back to my physical body, I could hear the pounding hooves of their horses coming closer. I had a premonition within my deja vu, that if I continued to stay in the astral and relive my approaching past life murder, I would die in the physical. My terror mounted as the violent event was about to re-ignite.

Suddenly, I felt a hand touch my shoulder. I heard Kim say, "I love you, Kathy." I shouted, "What took you so long? I was going to die out there!" And Kim replied, "I heard a voice say, three times, 'Go tell Kathy you love her.' And, I finally listened."

Kim's obedience pulled me back. Kim's obedience saved my life.

Chapter 12

Karen

As memory serves, my first meeting with Karen was at Reverend Richard Vallandingham's United Church of Revelations. Karen and I were in a Psychic Development class together. During the class we would do "practice readings" for each other. When it was Karen's turn to read me, her compassionate energy helped me feel safe.

Our friendship developed very quickly. Past lives? One fleeting recurring vision I had of us: two priests in long black cassocks driving a buggy in the night ~ fighting the icy, cold, Devil's wind ~ to go perform an exorcism ...

We would endlessly read each other regarding our various obstacles and dilemmas. Karen very accurately tuned in to Marc entering my life. I was so shy, reclusive. Karen's Gemini sociability and charisma helped me to open up. She really encouraged me to step out of my shell and flow. When I look back at how concentrated and intense my karma was with Karen, I now understand that I was in dire need of assistance. My Spiritual Teacher sent Karen to me as a gift.

Karen worked as a psychic at The Crystal Cave metaphysical bookstore during the period that The Crystal Cave was busted for not having a license to do psychic readings. Only Karen could turn such an unlucky, *inauspicious* event into a lucky, *auspicious*, prosperous shift in her fortune. Karen became well-known as "The Crystal Cave court case psychic." She was calm and eloquent throughout the trial which, in turn, made her rather famous! The whole event gave her an abundance of free publicity.

I thank my Spiritual Teacher for bringing Karen and I together in this incarnation. Karen helped me to tune into warmth, charm, being alive. Karen helped mold me as a psychic. Thank you for the many unusual, healing gifts I have received from you, Karen...

Chapter 13

Daman Choli
V-1 Green Park Main
New Delhi - 110016

So many hustlers trying to make a buck in India. Trying to get you to this shop, that shop, where they get baksheesh for bringing people in. Not my friend, Karthik. A pure soul, Sri R. Karthikian (as he preferred to be called) truly wanted to be of service.

While in Delhi, I was looking for the old Sixties-style Indian bedspreads. As always, my dear friend Karthik was "on the job" to fulfill my quest. Karthik brought me to a few shops he had found that had something similar to what I was looking for, though not quite right. As an afterthought, he walked me to a place down the street around the corner.

I can still recall the feelings, the atmosphere, the quality of light as I stepped back in time into Daman Choli, House of Rajasthan Arts and Crafts, Manufacturer of Traditional Ladies Garments. Visually starving, I was saturated in colour. My senses electrified. Entering into the creative region of Daman Choli was to change my life forever.

Their work is phenomenal. I have taken over fifty trips to India and I have never seen any shop that carries such high-quality, unusual, beautiful cloth.

My intuitive sense of the owners: Mrs. Pratibha Sarawat - elegant, satvik, quite careful, cautious. Pratibha takes doing business very seriously. Her husband, Mr. Inder Pal Sarawat - urbane, a bit of a Western energy about him. Inder Pal attended Delhi University where he earned his Bachelors Degree with Honors in English Literature.

Over the years, I have become very close to Pratibha, Inder Pal, and their incredible children, Supriya and Anmol.

Supriya received her diploma from the National Institute of Fashion Technology and subsequent degree from Pearl Institute, where she met her future husband, handsome Gaurav Monga. Fluid, flowing, exquisitely sensitive to all the beauty of God's Magnificent Creation, Piscean Supriya is carrying Daman Choli into the future with her own particular brand of creative genius. Her couture: Rajasthan meets Bollywood! Pure genius! I see fame in Supriya's future.

Anmol has a Bachelors with Honors from Delhi University. In his onward and upward career path, he received his first position in 2011, when Anmol joined Fluor Corporation, working in Engineering. A side note about Anmol: as a psychic, to my delight I have found Anmol to be one of the most intelligent, interesting conversationalists I have ever met. Anmol can cover a vast array of different subjects with clear, concise thinking combined with great sensitivity and diplomacy. His mind is most unusual. His work continues to evolve.

One of my favorite pastimes with Inder Pal is digging into his collection of embroideries. A journey through the past to the

Rajasthani village women pouring their souls into their personal diaries of textile poetry. Inder Pal and I are totally *tuned-in* to each other's love of these precious treasures.

In one of her previous incarnations, perhaps Pratibha was a female guru, beloved of her devotees. In this life she remains, as ever, pure spirit. A true channel of the Divine Mother.

And how do I bring Bhori Ji into this picture? Bhori, a homeless dog fending for herself, living on the streets in Green Park, adopted the Sarawat family. She hung around and hung around their shop until they realized she was theirs. Bhori loves roaming about Green Park with Inder Pal and I heard tell when Inder Pal gave up cigarettes it was Bhori who became sulky and depressed, grieving the loss of their early morning "ciggie walks." Bhori is so beautiful - a deer in her last life? She likes to chase cars, clearly tamed only by the family's love.

The Sarawats and I have shared many meals. Pratibha's churned butter, homemade yogurt, handmade chapatis...Divine!

We have bared our hearts. Absorbing Pratibha's tales of her saintly mother. I wish I could have met this noble soul! I remember Inder Pal's proud, stern father - the true patriarch of the family. Before really coming to know the Sarawats, I would see Inder Pal's father lying in the open air courtyard on his rope bed, overseeing all and sundry activities with his fierce eagle eye. Commander-in-chief. The protector.

They have blessed me. "In the Dream Time," they are my family.

Traveling is one of the saddest pleasures of life.

Madame de Stael

Chapter 14

Indian Arts Corner Galleria
30, Sunder Nagar Market
New Delhi - 110003

After satsang, in the dusty dirt parking area, a wild, burly, proud, Traditional Sikh taxi driver highly recommended a vegetarian South Indian restaurant, the Sagar Ratna. Back then, the Sagar Ratna was located in Delhi's Lodhi Hotel. As we walked in we saw that the Sagar Ratna possessed a fiery opulent altar emanating sparks of gold, dedicated to India's beloved Lord Ganesha Ji.

The restaurant bustled with business. Very prosperous! But, I digress. Let's talk about the food! Their dosas were fantastic! Abundant fresh coconut chutney. Hot, delicious sambar. Our meal ended with one of their specialties, South Indian coffee. With complete mastery, our elegant waiter prana-ized our coffee, by pouring it back and forth, cup to cup. Marvelous!

After lunch, we decided to check out vendors in the hotel. Amy went off to explore while I went into a shop close by. Walking through the door, I noted how peculiar it was that the lights weren't on. The owner seemed like a cool guy, yet something was amiss.

Why were the lights off? I can't stand being pushed to buy, but his dark shop had the queer effect of a damp funeral parlor. I was drawn to a lovely painting of Lord Krishna that the owner's Scandinavian girlfriend had done. Not for sale. Nothing else in there moved me. Nervously counting the seconds until I could get out of there without hurting the poor chap's feelings when, mercifully, Amy appeared. Such a sad, strange sensation . . . mentally blessing this man as I walked backwards out of his shop…

On a brighter note, Amy was very excited about her new discovery, Indian Arts Corner which, although right next door to "Mr. No Lights," could not have been more of a contrast. Retracing that first memory of entering Indian Arts Corner, I recall a small, immaculate space, radiant with Light and Energy. The shop's owner, Mr. Vijay Kumar Gupta, introduced himself to us with great warmth and charm, making us feel extremely welcome and at home. Vijay commanded one of his servants to bring us chai. Exhale. We sat down and relaxed, drinking lovely, hot Indian tea out of beautiful china, while playing with tray after tray of jewelry, much of it designed by Vijay, himself. Rainbow moonstones. Labradorite. Rubies. Sapphires. Rose quartz. A sea of Indian gems. Having a moment outside of time and space I thought to myself, "So this is how it was in my past." Slow down … breathe … linger over chai … enjoy the magical gems … *merge.*

Vijay cordially invited us to come visit his other IAC Galleria at 30, Sunder Nagar Market which contained, in part, a small, elegantly appointed Fine Jewelry showroom. Being Year of the Horse, oh how I loved riding down there in the auto-rickshaws of New Delhi. The wind in my hair! The wild, frenetic energy of the streets! I revisit this memory with waves of happiness: sadhus on foot with their sacred Brahma bulls, the symphony of honking horns, Amy fighting the wind to light a clove cigarette in the open-air rick, the crazed cacophony of city traffic. Delhi Hands!

After the hot, dusty journey we would stumble out of the rick, respectfully taking off our shoes, stepping up into the icy blast of the A/C, entering the marble coolness of the Indian Arts Corner, Fine Jewelry suite. Immediately given bottles of water as Manisha, Vijay's lovely Libran daughter-in-law, sends a boy out to fetch us sweet rose water lassis. Relaxing a bit, admiring their new creations. Pink sapphires. Yellow diamonds. Black diamonds. Blue topaz. African opals. Lustrous pearls. Electric Ladyland!

Bidding adieu to the jewelry, we climb the stairs to their Art Gallery to enjoy an elaborate vegetarian feast the Guptas have had prepared for us. Let me tell you, there's nothing like being hot, disheveled, tired in New Delhi, then sitting down comfortably to have Indian-Chinese veg food with an ice cold Pepsi. Divine!

I couldn't know, back then, the depth of my karma with the Guptas. Devout Hindus, the Guptas have taken me to aarti many times. Wistful recall of my previous incarnations as a young Hindu girl …

All of us love being nurtured and cared for by the Gupta family: generous, kingly Vijay, and his wife, graceful devotional Damiante, wonderful hosts Anju, and her husband Amit, Solving the Problems of the Universe, the mysterious Ajay; his beautiful wife, Fine Jewelry designer Manisha, and their charming, well-behaved children Yashaswini and Chaitanya; Hanuman's own Pramod; kind Lal.

And, Virinder Ji, of course!

Venerable souls, all. Infinite Blessings.

Never lose a holy curiosity.

Albert Einstein

Chapter 15

DOMA
Copper Brass
No. 12 Tibetan Market, Janpath
New Delhi - 110001

Reconnecting one evening at our hotel, Linda Ji and my sister, Cristina raved about a woman they had met on Janpath in the Tibetan Market named Doma. Listening to them, I had a strong premonition: "I must meet this 'Doma,'" but it was not to be that trip.

Upon returning to New Delhi with Maureen and Amy the following March, we went down to Janpath Road. Once there, I gave myself one block in the Tibetan Market to locate Doma. If I couldn't find her right away I would give up the search.

Entering a quaint, old, out-of-time shop I saw a frail, elderly woman with short silky white hair, wearing a simple tunic and long skirt. I announced, "We're here, this is Doma." I can still bring up that moment of looking into her gentle yet piercing eyes that see everything, hearing her gruff yet not unkind voice. It was only later that I realized there was a prominent sign above her door in large letters that said, "DOMA." I didn't see that sign at all, that first day.

Doma was born in 1927, Year of the Fire Rabbit. I would say, perhaps, she's a Pisces or a Cancerian because I feel water when I'm with her and many of Doma's early memories of Tibet involve water. As a young woman, Doma left Tibet to go to India, settling in New Delhi to make her fortune.

Doma is a very remarkable person. Truthful. She doesn't play any mind games. Her feelings are transparent. She easily weeps when something moves her. She is the incarnation of Goodness.

Doma has a very curious establishment. It's deep. The structure of her shop is quite small and you may think you've seen everything after a quick look around, but you haven't. Doma has beautiful beaten copper objects, high and low, throughout her shop. She also has crystals, stones, and jewelry. At times, she has old bronze or carved wood ceremonial Ganesh pieces. She has malas and prayer beads and Tibetan singing bowls. But, mysteriously, looking around again in little corners, niches, nooks, are treasures I swear Doma has hidden, hoping the right person tunes in and finds them. Such beautiful things.

Being fond of us, Doma sits us down and orders one of her boys to go get us chai. We're in her temple now. Although invisible to our eyes, the Tibetan gods and goddesses surrounding Doma are sitting up, alert, as our visit with Doma begins (once again). It's a great honor to pass time with Doma in her sacred shop.

I'm quite certain that Amy was Tibetan in at least one of her past lives. When she met Doma, Amy wept feeling Doma was one of her many mothers. I had a psychic flash that Amy's old friend Shawn also had a karmic connection to Doma. Although Shawn's never been to India, I sensed her astral body with us at Doma's.

It was an answered prayer for me when my husband, Marc, got to meet Doma.

The Dalai Lama and my Spiritual Teacher allowed us all to find each other again in this lifetime.

Doma: "Of the Lord; belonging to God."

We choose our own destiny. I wake up happy every day.

Michael Minutoli
Self-proclaimed greeter of Laguna Beach

Chapter 16

Joanne: Artiste, Christmas Pixie Dust Angel!

Triple Capricorn, Joanne, is one of the few psychics I hang around with. I have no earth in my chart and I love, love, love her Triple Capricorn energy, because I need it! With all my air and water, when I get in trouble I am quickly thrust out into the middle of the ocean, so to speak. One of my favorite things about Joanne is her ultra-earth sign ability to help pull me back to shore.

Joanne calls herself a "bread and butter psychic." Simple, practical. Case in point: not realizing I was entering the "change of life," I would call Joanne during my horrible crying jags. I would defensively tell her that I was experiencing great sensitivity while Joanne repeatedly told me "I know you're sensitive but you're starting menopause!" Disturbed and scared, I didn't like hearing this. Worried, Joanne bought me an over-the-counter menopausal product to take nightly. Thanks to Joanne, within two days of taking it the crying jags stopped.

I met Joanne years ago, while working at the Crystal Cave. During that time I saw a friend of hers named Linda for a reading. Linda later approached me about teaching some classes. Although I knew Joanne had never taught before, she came right to mind. I told Linda, "I get the feeling that Joanne would be a good metaphysical teacher. Why don't you talk to her?" Joanne said, "Yes," and her teaching career took off!

Joanne started holding classes in her home. Later at the Crystal Cave, she taught her course, "Practical Metaphysics," for eight years. Her class included the subjects: stones, crystals, tarot, astrology, manifestation (long before "The Secret"), self-development, and psychic protection. Joanne's useful information, combined with her sensitivity and charm, made her quite a draw at the Crystal Cave. She was a natural teacher (carried over from her past lives, no doubt). Joanne had an impressive following: up to 55 people per class! It was perfect timing. Shirley MacLaine's first book had just come out; people were hungry. Joanne was hot!

In the great volume of this lifetime, Joanne has experienced many diverse chapters. I remember being with her in the parking lot of the Natraj restaurant in Laguna Beach, about to go to lunch, when the necklace she was wearing broke. She carefully gathered up all the stones, went home, and restrung the necklace in a completely new design. Typical Joanne! The breaking of the necklace that day was auspicious. Joanne went on, creating her own line of complex, beautiful, artisan bead necklaces. Her powerful, mystical pieces were worthy of the Goddess. A Joanne mermaid altar piece blesses me.

Currently, Joanne is making dolls. I personally feel that's a very poor description for her absolutely beautiful, etheric, museum quality sculpted creations. Joanne would be the first to tell you she goes through quite a struggle bringing these "beings" into the physical realm. She makes fairies, angels, and Santa Clauses in the true Saint Nicholas tradition. When Uranus in Pisces formed a sextile to Joanne's natal Uranus in Taurus, Joanne plunged into the mermaid realm.

When Joanne starts her dolls she puts a crystal in their heart chakra to bring them to life. As I said earlier, there's a real struggle calling them into being. They want to come in, but they are resistant. It's interesting to note that the fairies in particular, are very wily and difficult. Joanne isn't having the easiest time manifesting the regal, elusive mermaids, either!

Christmas at Joanne's evokes a true Sulamith Wülfing Yuletide. To celebrate the Winter Solstice in Joanne's home fills my cup to overflowing. Her magically illuminated tree, vegetarian feast, and pure Christmas Spirit set the tone of this Holy Time. After celebrating at Joanne's no matter how many Scrooge-like lower energies I encounter, I'm cool!

Joanne... "God is Gracious." She is: The High Priestess.

The High Priestess holds scrolls of arcane information in her arms. In addition, the moon crown on her head, as well as the crescent by her foot indicates her willingness to illuminate what you otherwise might not see.

Chapter 17

Reading in Bali

ll my reading tours start of their own volition. My reading tour in Bali was no exception, and one reading in particular stands out.

My client was a widow named Adrienne from England. Her Polish husband, Viktor, was an artist. Years earlier, they had taken a trip to Bali and Viktor fell in love with Bali's magical energy. So, they pulled up their roots and moved to Bali. For a time, Viktor and Adrienne were quite happy. Then, very strange things started happening. Snakes started crawling into their house, slithering up the walls, knocking Viktor's art down.

One day, as Viktor and his Balinese driver were coming home, they encountered a thick, long serpent on the road, blocking the progress of their car. The driver said, "I am Balinese. I cannot run over this snake." Ominous. A storm was coming.

Finally, the fateful day arrived. A wild native from the mountains broke into their home. Viktor was in one part of the house, and the rest of the family was locked in another. Viktor fought with this man, trying to protect his family. Adrienne heard Viktor's piercing scream as he was stabbed in the heart. The ambulance service was very slow and Viktor died in transit.

I felt a strong connection to Viktor as I tuned into him through Adrienne. The message I received was: yes, although we all have a destiny there are certain markers to warn us about what's coming. Viktor hadn't listened. So many snakes showing up... The snakes were messengers, trying to tell Viktor and Adrienne to leave while they could.

Viktor was born in 1953, the year of the Grey Water Snake and Viktor died in 2001, the Year of the Gold Metal Snake.

Adrienne said that the day of Viktor's cremation was very hot and oppressive. As I listened to her, I was psychically transported to the heat of his cremation.

A few days later, another client invited me to her home to do a reading. I was drawn to a photograph that she had. There was one very strange-looking man in the picture that was pulling me. Of course, it was him ... my poor, Polish artist, Viktor.

Chapter 18

Behloy Gulleze

I received a call from a woman named Behloy Gulleze wanting a session with me. Instantly I was repulsed by her name: BEHLOY GULLEZE. What a creepy name. But I went ahead and set up the session.

A few days later, she arrived at our home and I ushered her in to sit in the client chair to do our session. Behloy was a very slight, plain, dun-colored woman. She looked very indistinct. But that was just the way she looked; appearances can be deceiving. Her energy was another story.

Behloy proceeded to tell me about her mother. She said that a psychic her mother knew was giving her mother a car. Behloy rambled on and on about her mother and her mother's psychic. I was sitting in my Reading Chair listening to this tangled, codependent mess thinking, "How in the hell am I going to read this in a half an hour?!" I started inwardly begging for help.

Then my little reading room completely changed. Behloy had stopped her monologue. She stared into my eyes. She murmered, "Double . . . Mirror . . ." I was under psychic attack! Behloy was pushing to get in my head. The atmosphere around me was quickly .

..morphing … I felt sick. I mentally begged my Spiritual Teacher, "Help Me!"

The next thing I knew, I was catapulted through my reading room door, standing fifteen feet away in our living room. I don't remember walking. It was as if I had been "moved." I was just "there."

Somehow, I got Behloy out of the house.

The whole experience had totally blown my psychic circuits. I told my husband, Marc, that I had just had a session with a woman who was obsessed with me and that I knew she was going to call me this evening. I told Marc I was not going to take her call.

Sure enough, that night Behloy did call. Marc answered the phone. He looked at me desperately, psychically begging me to pick up my receiver. I shook my head. I had warned Marc earlier I wasn't going to talk to her again. So Marc quickly had to channelize his Gemini Rising and do some fancy footwork to get off the phone with Behloy.

The next day, Marc went to his favorite little coffee joint in town, enjoying himself with his buddies. Who came in but Behloy! "Cafe Tilt" was only ten by twelve feet! Marc hunched down on his stool, trying to make himself invisible while Behloy was holding forth to the group.

I never saw her again.

Chapter 19

Italy

𝕴n a dream, I was a young teenage girl in trouble with my family. My mother was sending me to Italy to live with my aunt. The dream shifted to me arriving at my aunt's hotel and I remember thinking how beautiful it was. As dreams will go, I was in the past, present and future. *Seeing*.

The black and white marble floor of the hotel lobby looked like a magnificent chessboard. As I stood upon a black marble square, quietly marveling at my surroundings, my cousin came to take my bags. As if at a distance, I knew that I was going to marry him and that I was going to be happy. He gave me a small, thin, ivory cameo carved in the shape of Italy. I would carry his gift as a talisman for the rest of my life.

The lobby was teeming with foreigners. There were Negro guests in the lobby. I was quite aware in the dream that they were "Negroes" and not "Blacks" as in the future 1960's-'70's timeframe.

The hotel was a cool, happening place. I loved it . . . Fortune had smiled upon me.

I awoke with a wistful, nostalgic feeling.

Every event regardless of how bitter and unpleasant it may seem, is a direct expression of Divine Will, and it contains the seeds of higher good.

Pandit Rajmani Tigunait, PhD

Chapter 20

Amethyst Cross

I dreamt I had an amethyst cross and when I held it I levitated. I remember gazing at the cut of the stones, the beautiful clarity of the purple amethysts in my palm as I practiced ascending. Until finally I let go and flew out of the room and into the sky while holding my beautiful, of the saints, amethyst cross.

Chapter 21

The Schoolroom

𝕴n the dream, I was in the ocean with my mother. A tidal wave was rolling in. My mother was not afraid. She dove into the wave. I was really scared but I dove in after her. The tidal wave didn't kill me. I didn't die! I came up through the ocean into a one-room, log cabin schoolhouse. I was sitting at a little child's desk. It was a very sunny, warm, beautiful day. As I sat alone in the schoolroom, a Voice talked to me, reviewing my life.

The Voice asked me the question: "Kathleen, how long will you be following _____ through the National Parks System?" And even though it was a dream, I knew immediately what it meant.

The Voice was trying to tell me it was time for me to truly let go _____ and get on with my life. Upon hearing this, I remember feeling great repentance, surrender, and peace. I was so, so happy I had another chance to begin again. We so seldom have the feeling of a new beginning. In this dream, I knew I had another day to really be ALIVE.

After this dream, I met my husband-to-be, Marc, who in turn introduced me to my Spiritual Teacher. My life began again, just like the dream foretold.

Use the world as a training ground for sacrifice, service, expansion of the heart, and the cleansing of emotions.

That is the only value it has.

Sathya Sai Baba

Chapter 22

Atlantean Colour Machine

J dreamt that Kim came to me and showed me what I can only describe as the Atlantean Colour Machine. She warned me in the dream not to walk through the rays of colour because they could kill me.

Chapter 23

The Queen of Pentacles

Over the years I've had many Tarot decks ~ my favorite (in this life) being the Aquarian Tarot. But something happened repeatedly with the cards that disturbed and unnerved me.

When I would break and shuffle the cards to make them my own, I would find the King and Queen of the same suit, say Clubs, together. A random occurrence? It wasn't. It happened again and again and again ~ the King and Queen of the same suit together. They wanted to be together. Like they were alive.

I also found that if I "over-read" myself with the cards ~ meaning I kept asking the same question of the cards ~ they would attack me. The first reading would be informational, accurate. The second reading, fairly accurate yet somehow, a bit edgy. But by the time I'd asked the same question about three times, the cards would turn on me and give me a dark and disturbing reading. It didn't take a genius; I was provoking the cards and I knew it. Over-reading (of any kind) kills the energy, distorting the truth.

To this day, I still own some beautiful Tarot decks, but I leave them alone. I just admire them. I have a great reverence for the cards. I respect them. And because I crossed the line with my cards in the past and got smacked down, I fear them. In a spooky way. The "Lightning Struck Tower". Awe.

I had a teacher in high school, Frank Ellis: a very cool Scorpio, Moon in Aquarius, Leo Rising, intellectually stimulating, wire-framed glasses hippie. I would go visit Frank and his wife, Rose, at their home. Rose was an artist who did exquisite oil paintings. Their home was astonishing, full of art and meditation corners. A lovely, introspective, atmospheric place. One night, I asked Frank to give me a Tarot reading, and he kindly laid out the cards for me.

Frank gave me a ten card spread using the classic Rider deck. I was covered by the Ace of Wands. I was crossed by the Two of Wands. Above me was the Three of Wands. Behind me was the Four of Wands. Beneath me was the Five of Wands. Before me was the Six of Wands. Me in the future was the Seven of Wands. Influences around me were the Eight of Wands. Hopes and fears were the Nine of Wands, and the outcome of my reading was the Hierophant. Frank said, "Wow! Whatever your question was, it's gonna happen!" It truly was the Tarot reading of a lifetime. As I recall, I was asking if I was going to experience enlightenment. I could not know then that Frank's reading foretold that in about twelve years I would meet my Spiritual Teacher, to show me the way Inside.

... deja vu, past life sanskara, the Gipsy card reader traveling with my tribe. Remembering this brings up tremendous emotion and energy within me. My vardo, my colorfully painted, beautifully carved Gipsy caravan, hastily cleaned up and made presentable to do a few readings ... a turn of the coin, cross my palm with silver ... before me and my mate would break camp and load up, pushing our horses to flee to yet another town, village, province, with our hastily made money from my readings.

... my well-worn deck of cards ... by touch alone I could tell what many of them were ... the keys to my fortune.

Chapter 24

The Crystal Cave

I used to run into Karen Tate down at Reverend Dick's United Church of Revelations. Karen and her significant other were the co-owners of a metaphysical bookstore in the city of Orange called The Crystal Cave. The Crystal Cave was in the back of a shopping center in a small, intimate space. The Cave was an extremely atmospheric, cozy, Wicca-ish place.

The Big Man had told me to get a job at a bookstore in order for my destiny to unfold. Although I was very shy and scared of rejection, I approached Karen Tate about the possibility of working for her at The Crystal Cave. Karen and her partner meditated on whether or not I should come into The Crystal Cave Family, and received a "yes." I had successfully followed The Big Man's instructions.

Eventually, Karen and her partner moved the store to a much bigger space in the front of the shopping center. At The Cave, I did readings and worked behind the counter. I was terrible at the cash register, often requiring assistance to finish ringing up a sale. Thankfully, they were very kind, supportive, and non-shaming. I made so many mistakes; I don't know how they were so tolerant and forgiving.

Karen asked me to write down my impressions of the new space. I wrote down everything I felt, including that there was something about the people next door, something not right. This proved to be a very accurate impression because, indeed, they turned in The Crystal Cave for not having a license to offer psychic readings to their customers.

Let me describe what it was like for me, being at The Crystal Cave. The reading corner was set up on a small platform with the reading table, reader's chair and client's chair. Many times while I was doing readings – *private, personal readings* – customers browsing in The Cave would sidle up and stand quietly nearby, trying to listen to the sessions. Beyond inappropriate!

The Cave sold candles of many colors: pink for love, blue for peace, purple for spirituality, red for passion, yellow for mental clarity, green for balance, healing, white for purity; powdered incense for ritual work, love potions, prosperity, increase in money, etc.; restorative oils – ylang ylang, frankincense and myrrh, vanilla, patchouli, amber, orange, strawberry, frangipani, and more.

There were natural crystals of all kinds, and huge, brilliant, clear quartz crystal balls. I loved to hold these grand quartz crystal balls in my hands and practice scrying. They were very cool – even cold – to the touch . . . as I gazed into their fathomless depths. I longed to own them all!

The Cave also carried beautifully rendered pieces of jewelry from natural stones and crystals – amethyst, rainbow moonstone, rose quartz, smoky quartz, watermelon tourmaline, lapis lazuli, garnet, onyx . . . These magical pieces were infused with energy.

The art of The Crystal Cave included great, big, amazing posters of the Twelve Signs of the Zodiac laden with deep, complex symbolism. My cherished artiste featured at The Crystal Cave was the venerable, true queen of esoteric art, Sulamith Wülfing.

Throughout the day, New Age music played at The Cave, my favorite piece being "Mother Earth Lullaby." Very haunting, Moon in Pisces, melancholy. Karen and her partner and I were all born under Pisces Moon, and there were times at The Cave when the Piscean Energy was sublime, divine. I would feel literally blissed out on the watery, Neptunian waves.

Somehow, Karen Tate reminded me of England's Anne Boleyn with her long brunette hair, dark brown expressive eyes, beautiful pale skin, the endless line of her elegant neck, her slim tapered, bejeweled fingers. This impression about Karen came to me frequently.

At times The Crystal Cave was just a metaphysical bookstore. At intervals it transcended itself and became a vortex, a region, a place beyond this world.

Two books I happened upon at The Cave were Moon Magic and The Secrets of Doctor Taverner, both by Dion Fortune. As I recall the feelings these books brought up in me, it seems during my time at The Crystal Cave I was completing a karmic account with an old, British psychic society from a previous life. (Connected to Dion Fortune and her peers, perhaps?)

An interesting mélange of characters frequented The Crystal Cave. One fellow, Aura Bill, was an unpredictable guest who never failed to stumble in drunk on his ass, whereupon he would read our auras. I loved Aura Bill's descriptions of our auric colours. For instance, Aura Bill rhapsodized about the "Krishna Blue" aura of one of the girls who worked at The Cave. I was always gleeful when Aura Bill showed up. Something was going to happen! Like it, or not, someone was going to get a reading.

There was a highly skilled professional witch who used to stop by. She would buy hundreds of dollars' worth of supplies for her spellbinding. I used to love to imagine her Working Altar because, believe me, this sorceress bought us out: twenty, thirty oils and candles at a time, plus numerous packets of our powdered incense, roots and herbs. I used to trance out and think, "My goodness, how many elaborate situations does this witch work on?" I would visualize her monumental altar and all the spell work she did to cover every aspect, every nuance, of her life... and perhaps the lives of others...? Scary! When this enchantress came into The Cave, she carried with her a wild, electrical charge ... the feeling you get right before lightning is about to strike.

This witch-goddess and Aura Bill were at the top of my list of distinguished psychic superheroes who came into The Cave.

Under the able care of Karen Tate, the Crystal Cave is now in its prosperous third incarnation, at 891 Baker Street in Costa Mesa.

The Crystal Cave: a moving spiral of white light, ultimately launching me into the orbit of my life ~ to go where I needed to go and do what I needed to do.

Merlin's beard!

Chapter 25

Aquarius Maud, Psychic Voyager

I met Maud while working at The Crystal Cave. Maud was an Aquarian, perhaps in her early 70's but that's just a guess. Maud was extremely psychic. She'd had many unusual, paranormal experiences and I was lucky enough to hear about a few of them.

In one of Maud's adventures, she astral-traveled over to Africa and was bathing native tribal children who were very ill with dysentery. When she returned to her physical body in her bed in California, she discovered she had brought an African insect back with her. (This bug was actually verified to have been unique to Africa!)

In another out-of-the-body journey, Maud traveled to an underground Black Magic Brotherhood. A diabolical warlock was writing an evil ritual on the wall. In her astral body, Maud went up to the wall and kept trying to erase the damned, immoral spell. As she did so, the other Black Magicians in the cavern became aware of Maud's interference and charged her!!! In great peril, Maud fled the chamber and barely made it back to her sleeping form.

When Maud's mother died, her spirit wouldn't leave Maud's home. Maud's mother had been fond of sewing. When Maud would come home from work, she would find needles and pins placed in odd positions around the house. Maud finally felt she had to do something about her mother not letting go and crossing over. So Maud did inner work, asking for spiritual help for her mother's soul to leave her home and get on with her sacred journey on the other side. When Maud came home that very evening, the place looked like it had been torn apart. Her mother had finally left, but with great resistance.

Maud was a very plain, nondescript-looking woman. From the outside you would never know that she was a true Psychic Adept. I've met many gifted people over the years, through my work. But quite honestly Maud was in a league of her own, a skilled traveler of the inner worlds.

Chapter 26

Mame

Mame was a gifted psychic who helped me to make a major karmic turn on the road during a very critical time in my life. When I met Mame, she was probably in her late sixties to mid-seventies but she was very secretive about her age. Mame looked like an old-fashioned Madam from a Western saloon. She was All Woman! Even now, as I remember Mame, a real Mae West-type energy comes to me. Mame was a bit plump with a huge bust and she had piles of red hair, usually worn in kind of a Gibson Girl, pompadour-styled loose bun on the top of her head. Despite her busty, Dolly Parton-ish, over-the-top femaleness, Mame had a royal presence.

When Mame entered a room, she would pause silently, regally surveying the crowd with her eyes, until she was properly acknowledged. Then, like a Queen, she would enter the room. At this moment, as I mentally visualize Mame, I do not see her in today's modern garb. I see her in a sequined, low-cut, saloon hall evening gown because this is the image that she projected so strongly. Mame loved men. And she always had some "oldies" on the hook, courting her, proposing marriage to her. I can't remember a single one of these relationships coming to anything. But Mame so enjoyed these gentlemen.

Mame was a very proud, very nurturing Capricorn. She was a true mother figure to me. I was very blessed that for some reason - only God knows why - Mame adopted me as her psychic child and worked with me for free. So I would walk around Costa Mesa, call Mame, and drift over to her apartment. We would have a lot of fun talking and she would give me readings.

One of the very special readings Mame gave me was a channeled message from a Being from another world. This beautiful Being asked me: "Do you remember when I used to read to you out of the Book of Life...?"

Mame also told me in another reading that I would know everyone I ever met in this life, and that I would understand everyone I ever met in this life... this was the gift that I carried over from my planet. No glory to me, I have to admit that over the years (and it's been many years since I knew Mame) this has proven to be true. Although I ruefully altered her statement to, "like it or not, I understand everyone I meet."

I had a friend, Avonlee, who had a truly tragic, difficult, broken relationship with her parents. Avonlee was a very late stage alcoholic in AA, who had had many horrific trips to the mental hospital. Mame was very good with Avonlee. Mame tried to guide Avonlee into facing that, for this lifetime, her relationship with her parents was finished, over. Avonlee really fought these impressions. So, Mame - in her practical Capricorn way - picked up her own phone and called Avonlee's parents during one of their sessions. And, needless to say, her parents didn't want to speak to her. Truly that call was worth ten sessions! But, that was Mame.

[Note to Reader: Avonlee's situation with her parents WAS the exception to the rule. Many relationships are salvageable. Avonlee's case was very unusual.]

Mame really wanted me to go with her to do mini-readings at a psychic faire, and being the shy, reclusive person that I am Mame had to push me really hard. But finally I surrendered and one fateful Saturday morning, I did go with Mame to do readings at a psychic faire. It was such a trip. Mame was up to her usual tricks of flirting with the elderly men who had come to her to get readings. With a twinkle in her eye, Mame gave me an encouraging, thumbs-up, "Come on, Kathleen, you can do it!" look as, one by one, after she was done reading these gentlemen she pushed them to come over to me for mini-readings. Oh, no! I had probably seven to ten (I lost count!) long-retired men come to have a session with me at my little card table. They were all depressed and they all desperately wanted more income. Try reading that painful energy for three, four hours! I was so worn out, I felt like I was drowning. And then at the very end of the day, a man in his early forties came and sat with me. Tim had spent a great deal of time with Bhagwan Shree Rajneesh at his compound. Tim didn't fit "here" anymore. He was having a terrible time readjusting to his life in Orange County. I could feel Plutonian energy take over to help me with him. It was so powerful. Tim and I could both feel the psychic transmutation that had taken place. Tim's physical body, mental body, and astral body were a working unit - properly reconnected. Tim was ready to move on with his life here.

It's curious to note, that in my memories, I often have thought I did many psychic faires. But in reality, I only read at the faire that one day. But the experience of that one day evolved into a core philosophy of mine and over the years I've told many of my clients, " we all have to do our psychic faires," meaning, we have to get our feet wet, we have to get started somewhere with whatever we're doing in life. Mame did me a huge service, pushing me to go to the faire that day.

Mame gave me an astonishing gift. One morning, when as usual, I was hanging out with Mame at her apartment - drinking coffee, having fun, getting impressions - Mame told me that a very powerful psychic was coming to town and she wanted me to get a reading from him. Being psychic, myself, I had a lurch of fear shoot through my body as she talked about this man. I was scared, scared, scared (of course, I was having a major premonition)! I said, in my best wheedling, cajoling, run-away voice to Mame, " I don't have the money for a reading. I can't see this man."

Mame calmly came back with, "You don't have to pay him. I'm going to talk to him and arrange it for you." I said, "Well, I don't drive. I can't go see him, I don't drive."

"Don't worry," Mame said. "He's going to come to your house." I thought, "Oh, God!"

Chapter 27

The Big Man

There was no way out. Mame's logic had me cornered. It was my destiny to see The Big Man. Our appointment was arranged. He came to my house and knocked at the door, and when I opened the door and looked at The Big Man, I was stunned. You'll be surprised to hear that The Big Man was a very, very big man.

One of my outstanding memories of him was the lack of definition from his chin to his throat. Perhaps this translates as a huge double chin but, to my mind, it made The Big Man look like a huge, walking amphibian. He was neatly dressed ~ I think in a suit ~ and he had very cold, piercing eyes. But The Big Man wasn't cold, he was *intense*.

I was in for another shock. My "reading" with The Big Man lasted, probably, all of ten, fifteen minutes. He didn't waste a second; he got right down to business. He told me he was there to "kick my will". I intuitively knew what this meant and I got a jolt when he said it. He gave me a few brief case histories of his, whereupon he had kicked the wills of others who were flailing, failing in life. The Big Man told me I had a tendency towards melancholy, great sadness, that I would have to address, work on, the rest of my life. He told me that I should be working at a metaphysical bookstore and that I would probably meet my husband, either at the bookstore or at the beach. The reading was over.

I only saw The Big Man one more time. I was at some metaphysical event with Mame, of course, and The Big Man was there. He came up to me and seemed to do some kind of a scan, looking at me. He said he was doing a check-up on me. By then, I was working at the Crystal Cave. The Big Man was happy I had taken his life prescription to heart, and I felt a warm, loving energy between us as we said goodbye. Shortly after our second encounter, The Big Man died.

To The Big Man, wherever you are in this vast universe, I love you. Thank you for everything.

Chapter 28

S. K. Tripathi, Vaastu Palmist

On our last morning in Jaipur, I was drinking cup after cup of chai, sitting with Maureen and Amy in Maureen's hotel room and I had one of those lucid thoughts that we have: "You're sure drinking a lot of tea, Kathleen. You know you're really gonna have to go pee." I quickly filed that thought away and went back to my deep enjoyment of the plentiful chai.

Soon it was time for Amy, Maureen, and I to get in the car with our host, Ajay, and our driver and leave. As we were driving, feeling bumps on the road, I thought, "Oh, my God, I've got to go to the bathroom (just as I'd predicted earlier)." I said, "Ajay, please tell the driver to pull over anywhere. I'm used to these funky Indian bathrooms. I'll use just about anything." But Ajay kept talking to the driver in Hindi about looking for a "good" bathroom. This went on for several long, excruciating minutes. I was totally panicking. I was going to wet my pants! "Please, Ajay, please! Tell him to stop the car! I can handle the worst urinal that India has to offer." But, nooooo! Ajay and the driver continued consulting about trying to find a decent bathroom. It was beyond awful! I thought I was going to explode. Finally, Ajay and our driver spied a courtyard that held a restaurant and museum on its grounds. As we pulled up to park, I jumped out of the car, ran into the museum, and mercifully, mercifully, mercifully used the bathroom. (That'll teach me to drink

6, 7, 8 cups of chai before a big road trip in India. Of course, I was "blissed out" after using the bathroom.)

The bathroom I used was in a small, quaint museum which had displays of old Indian military uniforms. When we walked out into the courtyard, Ajay decided that we should stay for a nice, open air lunch. It was so wonderful to sit down and relax after my ordeal. The museum, the courtyard, the waiters wearing their old, traditional, beautifully pleated, Rajasthani turbans . . . I began to have that old, familiar sensation that I enjoy so much. I was starting to travel in time. This was all deja vu ~ things already seen before.

Several feet away from us, to our right, I noticed a palmist doing readings. I studied him carefully and got a good feeling. I whispered to Amy, "That man's heart is in his face. He's a good person. You should get a reading from him." Subtle, psychic, Pisces Ajay picked up on the secret exchange between Amy and I and quietly arranged for Amy, Maureen, and I to get a reading from the palmist, as his gift. When it was my turn (and I wanted to go last), I felt very shy sitting with the palmist. I hardly ever get readings from anyone. If there's one thing I've learned over the years, you can't be too careful about who reads you. But I liked this man and I surrendered to the moment. Here are some of the impressions he gave me. He told me that my husband Marc's book would get published (it did). He told me I could die whenever I wanted (I found this impression strangely comforting). And he talked to me about doing Pranayama breath work while walking through dewy grass early in the morning. He was such a sweetheart; I loved this man.

Here are some curious, karmic things to note about that day. It was my fate, my destiny, to drink all of that chai early in the morning, which allowed the Spirit of Destiny to pull us to the palmist. And then the story within the story: our palmist had a brother who was the regular palmist at the restaurant, but his brother couldn't make it that day and he took his place. The workings of this whole experience were so intricate, so precise. And as I said earlier, the restaurant, the museum, everything there in that courtyard harkened back to a previous life in Jaipur. (Was this our life?)

Sri Sri S.K. Tripathi Ji, my dear Palmist of Jaipur, I pranam you and blow you a kiss across time and space. Thank you!

There is more to life than increasing its speed.

Mohandas Gandhi

Chapter 29

Readings at Marina Shawn's

Shawn, Amy's old friend of many lifetimes (perhaps I knew her, too?) used to live upon acres and acres of drop-dead beautiful country in Cazadero, California. Amy and Shawn were born the same day, the same year, two hours apart. They both have Moon in Capricorn, although Shawn's Ascendent is very close to Taurus – more of an Earth energy happening in her chart.

For several years in a row, Amy and I would make the trip up the coast to go see Shawn. It was a long, long drive. Just like the Canned Heat song, "Going Up the Country," I could actually feel when the Northern California energy, which was quite lovely, morphed into the grand vortex of PURE NATURE. It was wild! One time, as Amy and I were driving to Shawn's late at night, we even saw a red fox by the side of the road.

Back then, there were no clear markers to the dirt road that led down to Shawn's immense acreage. Shawn had put up a few balloons to let us know where to turn and we slowly navigated down the steep, dirt hill. During that time, Shawn was living part-time in a small Airstream trailer and also in her beautiful, unfinished house which was a few feet away from the trailer. The trailer served as a kitchen, dining, base of operation and Shawn and her children slept in the unfinished house. I loved that little trailer, which I fondly called the "Yellow Submarine." Amy and I slept in the trailer whenever we visited. The trailer had a fold-out Formica booth-like dining table and a window right next to it looked out to the glorious view of Shawn's forest. It took me years and years to finally get the bottom, intuitive line of why people in that area almost never leave - to travel, to go anywhere. It is so breathtakingly beautiful there, that the beauty does a number on their minds. In a strange way, it breaks them. They find it almost impossible to leave.

Somehow, in its usual, mysterious way, reading tours started developing while staying at Shawn's. Clients would come see me in the beloved "Yellow Submarine" Gipsy caravan trailer and sit across from me in the small dining booth for readings. It was so raw, so "get-down" to see people for readings there. I loved it! It seemed that only my true-bluest clients would come down to Shawn's (and when I say, "down," I am visualizing going down that hairpin, sheer drop of a road into Shawn's wild, magical kingdom).

One time, Amy and I had received notice that our Spiritual Teacher was coming to Northern California and we raced up the coast to see Him. (Shawn had graciously told us we could stay in her trailer instead of renting a motel room.) Our Spiritual Teacher did not come; it was a false rumor - but there we were at Shawn's. Shawn had two young men on her property who were doing a three-day Vision Quest while we were there. I was psychically thrown into the wildfire vortex of a reading tour that instantly manifested for me. I was enchanted, deeply charmed by this turn of events. So I did the readings that were brought my way by the benevolent forces of the universe, the powers that be, and feeling a deep appreciation for *how things work.*

Eventually, Shawn's old soul mate, Michael, completed her beautiful two-story house and she was able to move in. Sadly for me, The "Yellow Submarine" is no more. But when I look back at those days, a warm wave of happiness comes over me. Shawn would feed Amy, her children, and I, delicious vegetarian meals, fabulous coffee with real cream, and organic chocolate truffles. And, I know I keep saying it was breathtakingly beautiful, but there really is no other description that fits. It was like I was starved for the deep country experience, and I didn't know it until I was at Shawn's. Her small, perfect, old Airstream trailer - my beloved Yellow Submarine - was a jewel in the crown of this perfect experience.

One last, amusing note about my reading tours at Shawn's ... During one of our trips, Shawn had several people in mind to see me in the trailer for sessions. None of them came - not one. But meanwhile, my regular clients were trying to find me, and my husband, Marc, kept referring their calls up to Shawn's. It was so funny to be doing one phone reading right after another at Shawn's during the time that had been allotted for her people up in Cazadero. I could tell it blew Shawn's mind - the twists and turns in the life of a psychic. There's no getting it.

I'm truly blessed and humbled by my time with Shawn. The last time I saw her was right after darshan and Shawn and her daughter, Hannah, served Amy and I absolutely heavenly, homemade strawberry shortcake with her famous coffee and thick cream. Beyond the beyond!

For Shawn's Spiritual Teacher and my Spiritual Teacher to arrange our coming together was no small thing. I can almost see how they bent time and space to do it.

Chapter 30

Wrong Today, Wrong Tomorrow

Ɉ once worked with two sisters who were in deep crisis. They called me daily. During every phone session, I would try my very, very best to attune myself to their horrific circumstances and help them. They were very appreciative, very sweet and very kind to me. Then they would call me the next day (and the next day, and the next day, and the next day). Upon their call the following day, everything that we had talked about the day before had shifted. Not a little, hairline fracture shift, but I'm talking about a huge point eight Richter scale earthquake shift! What could I do?

So, after brushing myself off and praying for guidance (once again), I would tune in to the new crisis scenario. And, as always, the sisters were very grateful for my help. This went on and on and on. My best efforts to help them were dramatically negated by the following days' new events.

So . . . I began to desperately cling to Principles and Intentions in these sessions ~ their inner moral fiber, so to speak. My impressions were so drastically wrong that I would spend the bulk of each of these phone sessions desperately trying to show the sisters that all that really mattered in their decisions was the purity of their "inner intention." And although, of course, this was obviously true, I was falling off a cliff with only a shred of a rope to hang onto. But still, they were so sweet to me. They never pointed fingers and said to me, "But Kathleen, that session yesterday (and the day before and the day before) was wrong! Inaccurate! And did not apply!"

Obviously, I was learning a lesson. There's a saying in Recovery, "Ego is not my amigo." Good Lord, was that true here! I was so humbled by my *wrongness* and their *kindness*. And, as you can imagine, with just the smallest shove I could have easily gone into acute humiliation. But somehow, thank God, I didn't. I finally realized that the sisters were hanging onto me to try to fill their empty tanks with love and strength and, if nothing else, I did play a small part in their "keep on keeping-on" in the face of their terrible problems.

In all my years as a psychic, I have never been so "wrong." I'm still sorting out this experience. But the fact that the sisters held on to me with such love and trust gave me a gift in my "wrongness" that will probably take me a lifetime to process.

Chapter 31

My Psychic Mother, Dorothy ~ Gift of the Gods

y mother, Dorothy, is very psychic, in a detached, impersonal, Aquarian Moon way. When I was younger, I would look at my mother and think that she used to be an Archangel many lives ago. Although my mother is a striking, beautiful woman, she has the stern, Saturnian turn of mind that I associate with the Lords of Karma. (Dear Reader, are you starting to put together that it's been a chilling experience to be Dorothy's daughter?)

Over the years, my mother would look at me dispassionately and pronounce, in her final way, "Kathy, you are exhausting that situation, relationship, etc., etc., etc." Oh, how I hated hearing this! Oh, how right she was! I got so tired of hearing these pronouncements from my mother ~ month after month, year after year ~ that I finally gave up and completely surrendered to the absolute truth of her intuition. And, of course now, many years later, I can comfortably help my clients as they beat the bejesus out of their relationships, their work, their dreams, etc., etc., etc. I know my way through this one, thanks to the guiding hand of my mother, Dorothy.

My mother used to read the Tarot cards. I used to say, "Come on, Mom. Let's make a pot of coffee and read the cards!" In those days, I was a smoker (loved it! loved it!), so we used to have a smoke-out and drink tons of coffee and read the cards. Two Tarot cards came up regularly in the readings my mother gave me. The first card, that often Covered me, was "Dreams come true, but you must wait". (And, yes, I got that card for several years - imagine that!). And the second card that often came up in the Tenth Position, was the King of Cups - a loving, kind-hearted Cancerian man. I know now that my mother's Tarot readings were pointing the way to my having to undergo a long period of painful and distressing lessons, as I was being prepared to meet my husband, Marc - The King of Cups.

I can recall my fiery Leo mother, with her lit cigarette smoldering in the ashtray, as she quickly laid out the cards. Often, my mother's readings were so piercing, I would feel as if I'd been socked in the solar plexus. The searing truth of her card readings stunned me. My mother's angelic wisdom, her detachment, her clarity made her quite a channel for information from Above.

My mother is a "Z" person. I don't recall her ever sitting me down and walking me through the steps of *how* to "let go". The writings of the brilliant metaphysical teacher, Catherine Ponder, filled in the rest (A, B, C, D, etc.) quite well for me. I have found Catherine Ponder's teaching of releasing everything and everyone to God in order to attract one's highest good extremely powerful and uplifting.

I always like to joke with my clients, "You may believe you hate your mother but she'll tune into you anyway." The bond between mother and child is one of the most primitive, supernatural, psychic ties any of us will ever experience in this life.

As I look back at my mother pounding me with her truths, with that raised eyebrow she used to give me, that look of exasperation, and as I recall the shame and anger it used to bring up in me, it feels like I'm looking back at another lifetime. With the acceptance of my mother's admonitions, my love for my mother flowed much more freely. I no longer had to defend my obsessive, clingy, torturous hanging on and, yes, beating situations to death, anymore. My mother was RIGHT. Right is right. So . . . ultimately, my mother psychically tuned into the fact I was born with a passionate, loving heart but that I would have to be okay with having and ~ perhaps even more importantly ~ not having the love and affection I so desperately wanted returned to me. Life is so much easier without desperation.

My mother has been my Living Spirit Guide in the inner and outer worlds. The feeling that there is a lack of love or responsiveness from this big, bright, compassionate Universe is an illusion. The more I experience the grace of surrendering my will in all situations, the more I know God's Love is all encompassing.

Thank you, Dorothy.

He that won't be counseled can't be helped.

Benjamin Franklin

Chapter 32

Psychic Sister, Cristina Marie ~ Christ Bearer, Angelic, Faithful, Star of the Sea

My sister, Cristina Marie, is very psychic in a dry, terse, Capricorn way. Years ago, I asked Cristina to tune into if I was going to marry. She said that I was either going to marry "a man in a three-piece suit" or "a long-haired, blond Hippie". That was the whole reading! I actually did have a Libran doctor (who wore three-piece suits) in my life whom I was very fond of. There was something between us (but what was it?). Doctor Libra never made his intentions towards me clear. I never knew where I stood with him.

Somewhere in this timeframe, I met my Marc ~ the long-haired blond Hippie whom I did marry. And, yes, I instantly knew where I stood with Marc ~ I was loved and cherished. No quicksand here. I used to say that I had to choose between a doctor and a healer ~ and I chose the healer. To this day, it still amazes me how Cris tuned into my karma with these two men in a one sentence reading!

In Numerology, Cristina Marie is a 9 Birth Path. Nines feel everything. It takes strength and courage to surrender to the supernatural gift of being a 9. I believe that 9 is the hardest of all the Birth Paths because it demands a dissolving of the ego. Purity.

Cris pours her intuitive ability into her love of animals - wounded, hurting animals.

Cristina Marie is the last of us six children, and we needed her! Her gifts, her abilities, her Light rounded us out.

Chapter 33

Psychic Sister, Kimberly (Cyneburg, Chineburlai) ～ Royal Fortress, Wood of the Royal Forest, From the Forest Meadow

My psychic sister, Kimberly, is a sensitive Virgo with the Moon in Libra. Kimmy cannot stand disharmony and conflict and she will go to all lengths to stop any energy she perceives as negative, intrusive. Kimmy needs hours of time alone to fill up her tank and handle the world. I believe Kimmy tunes in all the time; she can't help it.

When Kimmy was in high school, she started her own sorority. One time, her sorority threw a party, and during the party Kimmy had a psychic flash. She said "The fuzz are coming. I'm getting out of here." Indeed, within five minutes of Kimmy's leaving, the police did arrive!

Our sister, Cristina, had been searching for years for her beloved friend, Mark, who had disappeared off the face of the earth. Kimmy said he was not dead and Kimmy predicted the month and year Cris would hear from him. And sure enough, Cris got a call on her cell phone from Mark at the precise time Kimmy had foreseen.

Once, right before I was about to travel to India, I sat down with Kimmy and asked her if she had any impressions about my upcoming trip. She tilted her head to the side and gave me a very strange look and said, "You're going have some weird experiences over there." I know she saw the discomfort flash over my face, and she immediately tried to console me in her quick, Kimmy way. (Remember, Kimmy doesn't like conflict.) "It'll be all right! It'll be all right! Don't worry, it'll be all right!" But, nooooo, off I went over the sea, thousands of miles away, to a very peculiar, odd and disturbing trip to India. One icky thing after another happened on that trip. Kimmy was right! And from that time on, I have complimented her on that accurate impression and I tend to say, as I'm about to depart here and there on other trips, "I sure hope you get a good feeling this time!" In fact, on my very last trip to India, Kimmy told me I was going to have a blast. Fun, fun, fun! And she was right again. I had a fabulous time.

Kimmy is a bewilderment. She is so very vulnerable at such a core level that I don't know how she survives here in this rough old world. Kimmy is the High Priestess, shrouded in mystery. I will never completely know her.

Kimberly, the Royal Fortress.

Chapter 34

Aarti

Sanskrit
Aa: towards or to
Rati: right or virtue

Aarti is performed and sung to develop the highest love for God. Esoterically, connotes an intense attraction of the soul towards the Shabd.

It was the late afternoon of Maureen's March 13th birthday in Jaipur. Amy, Maureen, and Ajay had been spending the day as tourists, and they had just returned to our hotel to collect me. I'd been resting all day. Ajay was taking the three of us to Aarti at a Hindu temple and it was thirty to forty-five minutes before sunset when we arrived. I was wearing a long dress, suitable temple attire. Amy and Maureen were wearing pants, which women were not allowed to wear. Ajay, ever the subtle, secretive Piscean, talked quietly in Hindi to an Indian woman who was clearly in charge of important functions. This woman walked up to Maureen, took her by the hand, and led her up into a storeroom where she proceeded to put a proper Indian sari over Maureen's outfit. Needless to say, Maureen was in a bit of shock! Ajay had given Maureen absolutely no warning about what was about to happen. Maureen was having what I call, "an Indian Moment". Six or seven minutes later, Maureen reappeared dressed in her sari. American, Catholic Maureen on her first trip to India, having her birthday celebrated by the gods and goddesses. And Aarti began!

It was wild! The energy was electric in the temple. There was a festive aura of ecstatic joy permeating the atmosphere. I saw a Sadhu at the temple who weighed five or six hundred pounds. He was bare-chested, wearing a colourful lungi folded precisely and tucked firmly around his huge waist. I intuitively sensed my sensitive Sadhu brother was a prominent personage at the temple. This is where my memory starts to dissolve. Time was fading away. Like my Sadhu brother I, myself, am a big girl. So, I was completely astonished as the gods and goddesses that were being worshipped during Aarti lifted me off my feet and started TOSSING me around. I was up. I was down. I was on my knees. It was all beyond my understanding. The priests who were performing Aarti flung holy water from the Ganges at the crowds - so cool and refreshing. People were loudly chanting and singing. The Shabd - Light and Sound - untamed and free!

As we were leaving the temple, the sun was finishing its descent from the sky. Twilight was coming. The soundtrack from an Bollywood movie was playing. Vendors were out, selling their wares.

The dance ~ India.

Chapter 35

El Toro Road

It was 1986 and Marc and I had just had a $500 overhaul done on our car engine. As we were taking a test drive along El Toro Road, Marc stuck his left arm out the window, to signal a left turn, when a car swerved all the way across from the opposite side of the road and crashed into Marc's side of our car, under Marc's arm. Eerily, Marc had just promised me that morning that, starting tomorrow, he would wear his seat belt regularly. However, at that precise moment, if Marc had been wearing his seat belt, his body would have been crushed by the impact of the other car hitting his door. But as it was, Marc slid across the seat of our car and wasn't harmed at all.

Some off-duty policemen, who had been working out at the gym, saw our accident as they drove past us on El Toro Road and they called the Laguna Beach Police Station to send us help. I remember the policemen standing there (in their workout clothes) stunned that our car was totaled, yet we weren't even scratched. The on-duty police escort they had requested for us arrived and the officer driving the car took us home. We drove in silence. It felt like we were in a hearse. The energy was so strange, so absolutely quiet and still.

93

The day before the accident, a gentleman had called to schedule a session with me. After we scheduled, right before we hung up, I said, "Come 15 minutes later just in case I'm late." This was totally unlike me, as I am the very soul of punctuality. To my astonishment, Marc and I arrived home exactly 15 minutes late!

As I staggered in the door ~ white as a sheet, in the middle of our trauma, to do my session ~ I noticed that all the clocks in our home had stopped. All of them had stopped! I knew instantly, Our Spiritual Teacher had bent time and space to save our lives. I don't know how I got through that reading. I just stumbled through it on my inner knees, in shock and gratitude that Marc and I were alive.

Chapter 36

Chinese Astrology, Western Astrology

nce upon a time, on a beautiful, sunny day in Northern California, Lita, Shawn, and Amy were standing in a circle, talking. All three of these witchy women were born with the Moon in Capricorn ~ The Seagoat. Eerily, as I contemplated them, I saw an ethereal, blurry, Pan-like figure cavorting around them. Three Capricorn Moons had unleashed this ancient archetypal energy.

Andrea and Amy, both born in the Chinese Year of the Snake, were walking up the hill beside me after satsang, in India. Impossibly, they were both wearing that queer copper-green color that brunette, female Snakes seem to love. They had on their dark sunglasses (of course!), as they gazed at me intently. Their hypnotic double Snake energy tranced me out, which seemed to amuse them. As I walked up the hill, they glided alongside of me. Their unified, rolling Snake walk was so curious, so alien. Andrea and Amy were laughing at me a little, as I tuned into their strong, female, "snakeliness."

One evening, I was outside talking to my husband, Marc and my sister, Cristina. As we were talking, none of us were standing still. I had a moment of clarity when I thought, "We're all born in the Year of the Horse and we have to keep moving."

In 2001, I was doing psychic consulting for Michou Jewelry in Bali. As the sun went down after a long day's work, eight of us sat at a table for dinner. With the exception of three people, everyone at that table was born in the Year of the Rat! Looking around the table, I said, "Let's see you guys do The Rat." Instantly ~ as one ~ all five shape-shifted their "normal" features into the classic, hollow-cheeked, pointy rat face. While channeling The Rat, spontaneously they all started making toothy, snuffling rat noises. Astonishing!

A couple of decades ago, I went to an appointment with a Laguna Beach jeweler and something about his quiet, still energy reminded me of Neil Young. I asked him "Are you a Scorpio?" "Yes." "Were you born in 1945?" "Yes." "Were you born November 12th?" "No. The 13th." Close enough! Across time and space, I was having a parallel energy experience.

About eighteen years ago, before leaving India, I watched two Scorpio women sitting directly across from each other, eating dinner. The Scorpios were in a psychic tank of intense concentration, as they obsessed on each other's every word. Someone took a picture of them. When the photo was developed, believe it or not, their Scorpio stingers arced up above them, a dark astral shadow. You could see this in the picture. Creepy, weird, fascinating.

We are all on a wheel: a Wheel of Karma, a Wheel of Fortune, Wheel of the Zodiac, Wheel of our Chinese signs. Infinite wheels... Endless wheels...

Chapter 37

Kim Journeys on Without Me

aybe we were psychic twins. Maybe we were soul sisters. Whatever our connection was, it was brilliant. Kim - double Sagittarius, Moon in Aries, Chinese Year of the Horse, One Birth Path - was clearly one of my most challenging karmas.

Sadly, over the years, a distressing amount of friction had developed between us. I'm sure Kim perceived me as a coward. "Wimpy Moon in Pisces" were her exact words. And, I confess, I found Kim to be very self-involved, as if I were some sort of reflection of her. Not me. Not good!

We parted ways for several years. But, I missed her.

One day I sat staring at the sublimely beautiful picture of our Spiritual Teacher, inwardly begging for our reconciliation. Shortly thereafter, I received a letter from Kim! We tentatively started communicating again. In our correspondence, I urged Kim to go visit our Teacher in India, and unbeknownst to me she went.

My husband, Marc, over in India on a three week trip, was about to come home shortly. In those days, we were very frugal in our telephone communications between India and America. Close to midnight, I was lying up in bed in our loft, stiff as a board, electrical energy coursing through me. I couldn't sleep. Something was not right. Logic said Marc would not be phoning, he would be home soon. But psychically I knew he'd be calling.

The phone rang. I grabbed it and said, "What's wrong!" Marc said, "Well, the good news is Kim was here with me at the Dera. The bad news is, she just died in a plane crash leaving India." Marc told me that the previous night he had gone to the front office to see Kim off, before her flight to Saudi Arabia. The next morning, while he was reading the Indian newspaper there was an article about a huge plane crash. Marc experienced a wave of dread, returned to the office, showed the staff the article, and said, "That may have been Kim's flight." And it was. Kim had left this world.

For several days, after Marc's shocking call, I experienced Kim's spirit around me. At first, her energy was very sharp . . . clear . . . focused. Too intense. I said out loud, "Kim, you've got to turn the dial here. You've got to change the channel. This is too much for me." And she did! The frequency between us became beautiful, soft and blurry like an Impressionist painting. I would hear the quiet sounds of papers falling, books shuffling. It was Kim. For days she was with me.

Night after night her husband called me from Saudi Arabia. Grief-stricken, sobbing into the phone. He said, "Kathleen, every morning at 3:00am, I hear a door slamming in our house but no one's there." I told him, "It's Kim. She's trying to get you out of bed to meditate." After about two weeks, the door stopped slamming. Kim had let go.

Her husband told me Kim's girlfriend had a dream. In the dream, Kim was alive, full of Energy and Light. Kim's friend said, "I thought you were dead!" Kim answered, "Well, I'm not! But, I can't come back!"

For the next few years I felt depressed, fearful I was connected to the cause of Kim's death by urging her to go to India. It took me a long time to realize Kim's karmas were at the top of the Wheel of Fortune when she left this world. Things were going so well for Kim before she said farewell to the Earth plane. She was in a happy, peaceful place in her marriage. She had been taking her two children on many wonderful adventures all over the globe. They had high tea in London. They saw ancient Celtic crosses in Ireland. They went on a photographic safari in Africa, and saw cheetahs in the wild. They stepped back in time at the Egyptian pyramids. Kim had finally fulfilled her Sagittarian "long distance travel" destiny.

Kim had a love affair with wild weather. Her husband told me whenever they went away the weather would appear benign, calm. . . then out of the blue a freak storm would erupt. Gale force winds. Hale. Sheets of rain. Thunder, lightning. The elemental power filled Kim with ecstasy. She used to say, "Stormy weather outside, calm on the inside."

I've never really dreamt about Kim since she flew away. But Marc told me once, on December 6th, he felt Kim quietly enter the room and he said, "Happy Birthday, Kim." Marc always gets these treats, I don't know why...

Art is the only way to run away without leaving home.

Twyla Tharp

ཨོཾ་མ་ཎི་པདྨེ་ཧཱུྃ༔

Chapter 38

Vegetarianism and The Psychic Connection to Animals

've been a vegetarian since 1983. I became vegetarian for my spiritual path. It took a while for the morality of vegetarianism to catch up with me but when it did, it was shattering. It was as if God pulled a blindfold off my eyes and I saw clearly that animals are my brothers and sisters. Their souls are wearing animal bodies, but we are the same. My psychic ability, my intuition, regarding reading animals has been ten times stronger as a vegetarian. The eerie thing is I can tell that the animals themselves know that I'm vegetarian. I now realize that when I ate animals I saw their world through a dirty, distorted karmic filter. With that filter removed it was like I was given a "universal pass" to the animal kingdom: "There's Kathleen, friend of the animals. She doesn't eat us." This alone establishes intimacy, closeness, bonding almost immediately when I meet an animal.

Being a psychic, I see mad cow disease, swine flu, salmonella, mercury poisoning, etc., etc., as calling cards from the Universe warning us, exhorting us, to stop eating animals. Hard, harsh, but true. I know many people whom I believe, in their heart of hearts, truly want to become vegetarian but feel connected to eating meat with their families, their friends. Making a decision to walk this walk is a lonely choice ... or so it appears. The richness, the fullness of the Light is its own reward for karmic right action.

We are all here to evolve, to go *up the ladder* not down the ladder. The animals that are placed in our lives are our karmas, perhaps even people we've known and loved in other lifetimes who have had to go down into animal form to pay off their heavy karma. I have found being vegetarian totally speeds up the karmic completion between myself and my animal friends, and it helps them to keep ascending back to the human form, to realize God within.

Chapter 39

Papa Léon

Duke, my husband Marc's father, passed away many years ago. Marc's dad was a mysterious Scorpio. He was a very sensitive man but he was not easy to connect with emotionally. He had very high standards for how he wanted Marc to live his life. Duke had detailed plans for how Marc was to go about executing *his* ambitions and desires for Marc. Marc did not fulfill his father's dreams and this broke Marc's heart.

So...during a time in our life when Marc was trying desperately to process some of this endless pain about what he perceived as failing his father, Marc came across a powerful psychic ~ an African American voodoo practitioner, working out of his own metaphysical bookstore in Hollywood. Marc is very tuned in to readings and he had a gut feeling about Papa Léon. Papa Léon read Marc's grief and pain very accurately and here is what he told Marc:

Papa Léon said, "Go to the graveyard, Marc ~ any graveyard ~ take a white tapered candle with you. Try to find a tree or some secluded spot where you can be alone in the graveyard. Stick the candle in the ground. There is no need to light it. The candle signifies turning on the switch between the Earth plane and the Spirit plane. After you have pushed the candle in the ground, talk to your father. Pour your heart out. Say everything that you need to say."

Marc followed Papa Léon's advice to the letter. One day he went on his quest to the graveyard where his dad was buried. He was gone for several hours. Late that afternoon, early evening, Marc staggered in the door. He said the experience had been good, but traumatic. He looked like he had been to hell and back. His coloring was mottled and he had clearly cried and cried and cried. But after that day, Marc's universe shifted. The cross he was carrying became a lot lighter, easier to bear. I have never met a man who didn't carry a cross for his father, and Marc is no exception. Yet somehow Marc's crossing paths with Papa Léon and following Papa's prescription down at the graveyard was one of the biggest mental and emotional psychic healings I've ever seen Marc receive.

Chapter 40

Duel at The Eye of the Cat

t 3314 East Broadway in Long Beach, California is a Knockturn Alley-ish bookstore called "The Eye of the Cat". It was always a thrill to go there! One day when Marc and Amy and I went to The Cat, we experienced quite an event. As I recall, Amy was wearing a long orange batik caftan from Africa accompanied by several long, striking necklaces. She looked like a Mambo! After the usual browsing through the store and trying to get The Eye of the Cat's resident, de rigueur black cat to say "hello", our attention was diverted to a very bizarre spectacle.

A strange man in his mid-to-late thirties was walking to and fro in the middle of the bookstore, silently murmuring incantations and waving his arms about as he used his hands to create elaborate symbols in the air. He was tall, thin, and bony with stringy grey hair past his shoulders. He, too, was wearing a long, colorful batik dress and lots of jewelry. In fact, I know this is the reason I can always easily recall what Amy was wearing that day because Amy and this man were dressed quite similarly. Destiny? As this man (transvestite witch?) went about building his spell, the interior space of the bookstore was morphing into a negative vortex. The three of us silently exchanged a look: "What to do?"

Marc suddenly shifted into high gear and walked into the center of this freaky witch's creation. The energy was ominous. Amy and I stepped back. This was a duel. Marc strode through the witch's occult symbols. Marc was performing an *uncrossing*. With great force, power and concentration Marc mentally repeated a spiritual mantra at the Third Eye as he strode back and forth through the witch's construct. This made the witch crazy!

When Marc finished his walkthrough, the witch quickly took his turn ~ gliding about, redrawing his symbols. He was careful not to make eye contact with Marc. Although he was clearly agitated, frustrated, he acted like none of us existed. Marc advanced back and forth, back and forth, once again ~ breaking up the witch's peculiar, afflicted, psychic formula. This ordeal, this expulsion, went on for a long time. Finally, the witch looked confused and defeated. He gave up and quietly disappeared. The battle was finished and we left.

Chapter 41

The Séance

Many years ago, during my whirlwind time spent in the company of Reverend Dick Vallandingham at his United Church of Revelations, I'd made a Pisces friend named Ken. Ken was a long-haired, ponytailed bit of a hippie but mainly a professor type. Today he would be a paranormal research scientist. Most of the people in our "Revelations" group were going to be attending a séance that night and Ken asked me to go with him. I personally have never been a fan of spirit manifestation. Too scary! And it takes me a long time to recover when I have had encounters with beings that are deceased. So I said, "no" to Ken and we both went our ways - Ken to the séance and me, home.

During that time I lived alone and when I went to sleep that night, I woke up somewhere between two and three in the morning. Standing beside my bed was a 300 pound Swedish woman with gray braids pinned to the top of her head. I stared at her in frightened stupefaction. She looked at me grimly. I have a kind of blackout about the moments after that. No memory comes up. I think I just checked out to survive the spectral visit.

Later, in the delightful, blessed light of day I knew only one thing to be sure: the séance had come to me.

Eternity is ever in love with the products of time.

William Blake

Chapter 42

Dive

I was a black man working in a honky-tonk. Rich white people loved to come to the speakeasy when they were slumming. One night a fight broke out. Guns were firing. A bullet hit me in the spine. I don't know how I made it back to the little room I rented. I was lying in bed, dying. I was in love with my landlady and wished she knew how much I loved her. These were my last thoughts before I died.

Chapter 43

One Dead in O-hi-o

Many years ago, an acquaintance of mine had an unusual spirit experience. He felt one of the students who was killed at Kent State enter his body. I was fortunate enough to get to talk to him during this brief encounter. The spirit told me, the hardest part of his ordeal had been the shock of his sudden, unexpected death. He said that *certain lights* allowed him to come in and visit the physical plane at times. He seemed to have accepted his traumatic experience. He was very kind, very grateful to get a chance to talk.

Chapter 44

No Body

A long time ago I was sitting by the ocean at night, consciously trying to make contact with UFO's. I didn't know what I was seeing in the night sky but it didn't seem like anything was out there, yet I felt strange, odd, off, as if something bad was about to happen. Out of nowhere, I heard this horrible sing-song, disembodied voice repeat again and again, "I ain't got NO BODY that I can depend on" (a warped, twisted, sick version of the song by Santana). It freaked me out. It felt evil. I picked myself up and got out of there. My realization afterwards was, "Don't go looking for UFO's, Kathleen. If you're meant to see them it will happen naturally."

Some freakish being had sized up my vulnerable state and jumped in. I wasn't about to let this happen again. No way!

Chapter 45

Divine Intervention

I read the mother of a young man who was a real partier, a real drunk. I told her that her son was going to go to AA.

She came back to see me again and told me that, miraculously, her son was attending AA meetings. I told her to tell her son to check out a lot of meetings because he was going to find his wife in an AA Meeting.

Session 3: My client gratefully told me that, as seen in our previous session, her son *had* found his wife in AA. She was waiting for him. Another miracle!

It has been my experience that folks that have no vices have very few

virtues.

Abraham Lincoln

Chapter 46

A Grave Realization

When I was about fifteen years old I was very interested in psychic phenomena. Too interested. I was an open, naive, innocent channel. Not good. I was playing with fire and didn't even know it. Predictably, I started attracting negative spirit activity. Thus began my lifelong horror of spirit manifestation.

I remember sitting on my bed when suddenly it started rocking. I froze in fear. With a very weak voice I asked the spirit (spirits?) to stop it. AND IT STOPPED! I learned such a valuable lesson that day. I realized that although I had merely asked the spirit activity to stop, my request had been obeyed. My feeble, scared-to-death request had been obeyed. What would happen if I meant it, if I spoke with authority?

So, as a young girl, my two major realizations were: first "Respect the spirits, Kathleen, don't disturb them. Don't agitate them" and second, when something goes amiss psychically, command it to stop. Demand it to stop. Stay grounded. Hold your power. Hold your space.

Interestingly enough, many years later watching psychic medium, Chip Coffey on the show "Psychic Kids: Children of the Paranormal," I took note of Chip exhorting the children to find their voice with the spirits, to have mastery and command over themselves in these harrowing situations.

But back then, I just had me.

Chapter 47

Sally

In early elementary school I met a sweet, sensitive girl named Sally. Sally perceived some intuitive quality in me that allowed her to confide a secret. She told me that little balls of light would visit her every night. She was in awe of this experience. She cautioned me that I must never tell another living soul or the energy would die and she would lose her visits. Of course, I immediately told a few other children.

Shortly thereafter, Sally came to me and in a crushed, hurt voice confronted me for exposing her secret. Just as she had predicted, the energy was dying. Night by night, her astral "friends" were disappearing. I'm certain I burned with shame that day. I was mortified. I had betrayed Sally in the worst possible way.

The message has come to me, again and again over the years: spiritual experiences are meant to be kept inside, not rudely displayed. This traumatic event ~ my hurting Sally so deeply ~ became a nail in the cross of my childhood, never to be forgotten.

Chapter 48

The Lurid Affair of Madam Violata

his is one of the weirdest, most distressing cases the Universe ever laid on me. Normally, I have very clear "videos," as I call them, of my experiences. But I only remember fragments of this one.

I had a session with a woman named LaTanja. LaTanja had been receiving psychic readings that had gone terribly wrong. Her psychic, Madam Violata, had infiltrated and bored her way into every aspect of LaTanja's life. LaTanja said, "Kathleen, even at this moment, while you and I are speaking, I know she knows I'm on the phone with you." Under Madam V's warped "guidance," LaTanja had become estranged from her family and her marriage was beginning to disintegrate. It was time for LaTanja and I to get down and get to work!

Acting calm and in control, LaTanja began weaning Madam V of their connection and, effective immediately, LaTanja started making the necessary overtures to reconcile with her family. They could provide La Tanja with a natural force field of protection from Madam V. Safety in numbers. LaTanja's family was dysfunctional (whose isn't?) but they were her family. Madam V's compelling LaTanja to abandon her family was a violation of Universal Law. Very, very heavy karma.

Although LaTanja had an honorable husband, Madam V had been working on ending LaTanja's marriage. In LaTanja's past there had been a dark, mesmerizing man that Madam V was obsessed with. Madam V wanted LaTanja to have an affair with him so she, Madam V, could experience his energy through LaTanja. She pushed LaTanja hard to cheat on her husband and channel this sexual energy for *her*. Sick, crazy stuff!

LaTanja reclaimed her life ~ the life that Madam V had almost destroyed. LaTanja stayed with her husband, had a child, and remained connected to her family. LaTanja had finally come out from under being Madam V's psychic slave. With knowledge and spiritual power, LaTanja locked and closed the psychic door between herself and Madam Violata. Amen!

Chapter 49

Quarter of an Hour

I received a call from a client requesting a fifteen minute reading. OK, no problem, I did it. But after that fifteen minute session this man started referring people to me from all over the country for fifteen minute readings. To my shock, this went on for weeks and weeks. And I did them. One fifteen minute reading after another.

As suddenly as it began, the fifteen minute sessions ended. My intuition was that I had been bombarded with all the fifteen minute sessions to keep me sharp, focused, flexible. Whenever I come across a psychic who demands a major time commitment from a client, I mentally shake my head. There's no way out. Always and forever, readings are about letting go. Letting go ... letting go ... letting go. The avalanche of fifteen minute readings I went through ended up being quite the zen experience. Not controlling. Trusting. A gift.

There is no solution. Seek it lovingly.

Chinese Proverb

Chapter 50

Psychic Grandmother Bertha Cleo Gorrell Voigtlander

Bertha ~ Bright; Cleo ~ Glory of the Father; Gorrell ~
By a muddy stream; Voigtlander ~ Field of Roses

My mother's mother – petite, auburn, freckled Cleo – rose before dawn to wash, starch, iron, scrub, and endlessly cook for her husband and their eight children. An industrious keeper of the home and hearth on the earth plane, Cleo was also an extremely gifted psychic. I never met my grandmother in this world, but how I would have loved to have sat with her at her kitchen table, gazing into her pure blue eyes, sharing cup after cup of her famous cream and sugar coffee while she trained me in The Work.

My grandmother cut her children's hair by the phases of the moon. And in the *old gipsy tradition*, my grandmother was well-versed in how to interpret signs, omens, and portents. For instance, if you dropped a piece of silverware while you were with her, she might say, "A young man will be showing up at your door tonight." She could read all of these household auspices.

During one of my many troubled times with an old boyfriend, I went with my girlfriend, Vera Gail, to a metaphysical spiritualist church in Anaheim. I received a spot reading after the service from one of the psychics. She quickly deduced I was in trouble at home and she picked up that the danger was coming from him. She said, "Your grandmother is here to help you."

Driving home that night was utterly and completely surreal. The energy was highly charged, like right before a lightning storm. Vera Gail and I saw two little boys hitchhiking. I was so scared seeing these children alone on the side of the road. We picked the two brothers up and drove miles and miles to get them safely home. The night had a dreamy, blurry, unreal quality. The Twilight Zone.

When I got home, sure enough, my boyfriend was violently scornful, ugly. High. I heard a loud sound, like a baseball bat crashing onto a piece of wood furniture. Instantly I knew it was my grandmother revealing she was with me. Emboldened, I kicked him out!

On fire, it took me hours to go to sleep that night. But finally, exhausted, I drifted off. A pleasant, sweet, woman's face appeared to me out in the astral. My grandmother! She said, "Everything will be all right now, dear." I awoke with a jolt. I believe this all took place at 3:00am.

Grandmother, a January thirteenth Capricorn, was very superstitious about the number 13. My mother was born August thirteenth. My grandmother tried for years to get my mother to pass her birthday off as August twelfth. I believe thirteen is a lucky number. The old saying was that there were twelve apostles and one Christ -13.

Cleo loved nasturtiums. My mother, Dorothy, has nasturtiums growing wild throughout the year. She knows that this is her mother's way of saying hello to her, as a spirit.

My grandmother, Cleo, is the melancholy, superstitious, psychic aspect of me. She is *my ability to read signs and omens* as they show up … to interpret dreams, translate visions. Grandmother sent these abilities down to me through the Dream Time.

My grandmother predicted that she would not live to be fifty. As she prophesied, with one long, quiet exhale of her precious breath, she died in her forty-ninth year.

Chapter 51

Gift Psychic

new client, a woman in her late thirties to early forties, sat in front of me in my reading room right after Christmas. Suddenly during our session, she pointed to a plastic watch she was wearing and said, "Look at this shit I got for Christmas!" Okaaayyyyy, this is a curveball in the old reading, I thought to myself. I adjusted my scrambled mind to this new turn our session was taking and compassionately asked her how she felt about her unwanted gift. She told me that people did this to her all the time – giving her cheap, pitiful gifts. Somehow we got through the rest of the reading and I felt so sorry for her.

But our session stuck with me. I couldn't get her out of my head and I made a decision. I let it be known to all of my regular clients that henceforth, I was offering the free service of "Gift Psychic." And they sure took me up on it! I enjoyed this work immensely. It was so gratifying to steer my clients away from, if you'll excuse the expression, "acting out," passive aggressive behavior in the form of, shall we say, get back gifts!!! Needless to say, I did a little confronting.

One satsang I gave regularly during this time was, if you cannot afford to get a nice gift that truly represents honoring the loved one you are buying for, then get them (or make them) a beautiful card! Give them something you've made with your own hands, from your creative inner self! It really is your thought – your energy – that counts.

Dear Reader, you would be shocked to know how many of my clients (in my opinion) cunningly, pretty much *planned* to get their cards, gifts to their friends and families late! This issue came up again and again. Many of my clients freely admitted to me that they *wanted* to be late in their delivery because they were pissed at the person that they felt they had to acknowledge. Clearly, my work was cut out for me!

Oh, I so enjoyed my days as the Gift Psychic. I felt a bit like a combination of Miss Manners, Jane Austen, a personal shopper all rolling into a glorious crescendo of Charles Dickens' A Christmas Carol (a movie which never fails to reduce me to tears). I loved trying to turn my little, snoidy Ebenezer Scrooges into True Givers.

To me, the long and short of it is: For God's sake, if you're going to give a gift, do it right! Open your heart. Connect to the true essence of love you feel for the person you are honoring and you will find your way.

Chapter 52

No Water

J spent a few miserable years, off and on, at a local junior college. Over time, it became clear this experience was not for me. But meanwhile, during one of my "on" periods at the college, I had the following unusual psychic experience.

I met a beautiful, young Hippie boy. He had long dark hair, mustache, dark blue eyes. Without any effort he was just tuned-in to me. There's no understanding these things, really. I told him I was really depressed, that my life didn't seem worth living. He looked into me and with a stunning combination of mental clarity and keen intuition he told me, "You've gotten away from the Stream of Life, man. You're out on the rocks in the desert. You've got to get back to the Stream of Life."

His words hit me like a bomb. He was right. I was out in the dead, psychic desert of annihilation. So very, very far away from the water of life. How to get back? But it gave me something to work towards, a clear intuitive image of where I had to go. And somehow in that moment, as scared, shut-down and depressed as I was, I started to take the first step.

My Beautiful Hippie Sage was an Aquarius-Pisces. I believe he was born February 19th. He was so curiously perfect for me at that exact time, that exact moment of my life. With my Sun in Aquarius and my Moon in Pisces he somehow pulled all my worlds together and handed them back to me.

And I just had to take it.

Chapter 53

Spirit Guide Soiree

Karen invited my mother and I to an evening of having our spirit guides channelized for us. This event was held in the basement of a suburban tract home – a windowless, airless room with no ventilation of any kind full of smokers, smoking their brains out. I had to laugh at the Universe's Divine Sense of Humor, as I had just stopped smoking.

We all gathered close to the medium who was rendering spirit guide drawings. Her hand flew across the soft textured sheets of grey art paper as she used her fine pastels to psychically interpret her inner vision of the guide she was drawing at that moment. Each spirit guide drawing that she did was a revelation.

My spirit guide was a Spaceman and he had a message for me which she wrote upon the drawing – "I'll be back." No one else had a living guide that night.

My mother wept when she received her guide – Jesus! Everyone was blown away.

Wading through the sea of smoke and spirits, I was ill all evening I don't know how I made it through that trance-y night.

Possession of knowledge does not kill the sense of mystery.
There is always more mystery.

Anais Nin

Chapter 54

Alien Enneagram

isiting the Southwest, I was doing sessions at the beautiful home of Sol and Luna. Sol and Luna, brilliant, successful, gallery artists, utterly captivated my creative spirit during my time with them.

Daily, while preparing for my readings, I would look around their family room (which served as my temporary reading room) at photographs of their family. The pictures of Luna had a strangeness about them. Filing away my uneasy impressions, I would mentally shake my head and forget about it until the next day when I would gaze at the pictures again, before starting work.

During this reading tour, one of my favorite clients was a fascinating man whom I affectionately called, Cosmic George. George had been a widower and while his wife was alive, they had provided compassionate care to many foster children. For several years, George had been experiencing terrible heart problems. After George's wife passed away, he became involved with (and later married) a lovely woman named Sarah. In the midst of these vast, karmic, life changes, George began to spontaneously tune in to his alien root origins, hence the emergence of "Cosmic George."

As Cosmic George delved into his interplanetary past, everything in his life transformed. His heart, which had been literally killing him, now functioned beautifully. He ran up the side of steep hills with no ill effects. He had tremendous life force, abundant energy. Out in public, if people were acting out, being rude, disruptive, Cosmic George would put his mind to the problem, stop the negative energy, and bring the group under control.

Cosmic George's aura radiated purity and love. Reading Cosmic George was a gift.

The days flew by – at last! – I had completed my final session. Time for me to strike the set, pack up my crystals, and fly home in six hours. Sol and Luna were generously hosting a farewell dinner for me. I was visiting with Luna in the kitchen as she prepared our feast. We were talking about UFO's and aliens. Exhausted from all the readings, I was just sitting there relaxing, as Luna began to tell me a very personal story.

When Luna was a teenager in the Girl Scouts, her troop went for a hike. Mysteriously, Luna became separated from the rest of the girls. Looking up, she saw a UFO – a large craft, silently floating in the sky above her. Immobilized, Luna lost all track of time. Experiencing a strong longing to go up into the ship, she argued with herself. "Wait! I want to have children. I want to get married. No! I can't go!" I broke in, "Luna, I don't get that's how it went at all. I believe they told you 'No, you can't come with us. You're going to marry. You are going to be a mother.' I sense these were your Beings, loving you, missing you – family. I believe they told you it was not your destiny to join them."

Beginning to tear up, Luna looked at me and said, "Well . . . It's interesting, because when I take off my glasses . . ." She pulled off her glasses and I stared in astonishment into the eyes of a Gray. Limp with shock, I literally started sliding out of my chair to the floor. Now I knew why her pictures in the family room had unnerved me so. I quickly gave myself a stern mental command. "Get it together, Kathleen! She's trusting you with this. Act normal!"

That evening, Cosmic George came to my goodbye dinner. As the sun was setting, Cosmic George and Sol and Luna's teenaged son, Isaac, and I drifted outside to the pool. Cosmic George and Isaac gazed at me intently, with alien energy. They both began to assume strange positions. Yogi contortionists, indeed! Their arms stretched out. Their palms, open. Sending me healing energy through their eyes and hands. Suddenly, I got it! Of course! Isaac was part Gray! Exhaling, I relaxed and just let my Space Brothers send harmonic energy.

That night, at the airport, it was announced that my plane was experiencing a mechanical malfunction. My assigned seat was number 13. Thirteens have often been very lucky for me and I was hoping LUCKY 13 would come through for me, now! My luck prevailed. Finally, we were allowed to board. As Earth Time goes it was a short flight, yet I felt a dull sense of dread and apprehension, as the plane ascended into a dense energy field, flying straight up, pulling itself through the huge, magnetic vortex, in order to shoot over to California. The spiral caused by Earth Time hitting the strange, shifting permutations of Inner Plane Time had taken its toll. It was going to take me a while to get home to *my matrix* that night.

Chapter 55

Who Will Feed My Child?

A couple from the Middle East. Their little girl had just died. They were ritualistically laying out food for her daily. I begged them to stop "feeding" her on the other side. I told them it was magnetizing her soul to the Earth plane.

Such a tragic couple. If they could only see the pain and guilt they were creating.

I never saw them again.

Chapter 56

Astral Lecture

reaming, totally calm, confident, giving a lecture in an opera hall. I was not afraid. It was a full house.

In the background of this dream . . . a psychic I've known many years who had always judged me for not being ambitious. She did not understand I was happy with my readings, although I was not well-known.

Message delivered. I am doing what I am supposed to do. Some feeling of not being successful by other peoples' standards was left behind in the thunderous applause of my astral audience.

Gratefully Yours

My Spiritual Teacher, step by step, guiding me up to Sach Khand.

My beloved Marc, watching you toil away on your yellow legal pad for 5 + years, writing your book ORANGE SUNSHINE: HOW I ALMOST SURVIVED AMERICA'S CULTURAL REVOLUTION convinced me I could do it. You told me it was hard, and you were right!

Capricorno Luna. How many lifetimes have you been my scribe, recounting this old psychic's tales?!? Time for us to wind this all up, and leave this beguiling, mesmerizing planet behind! I not only could not have done this book without you – I would not have done it! Thank you! Thank you! Thank you! You have Blessed me.

My psychic Mother, Dorothy – I need you. Thank you for nurturing my soul and dampening my ego. Ric – Thank you for your endless love and devotion for Kimmy. Matt and Janette – Thank you for truly being family. Jim and Cris – Thank you for inspiring me with your creative genius. To my brother Mark, thank you for being my Hero. And to my brother Dave, thank you.

Maureen – Thank you for your compassionate Piscean support to always go within, and know, know, know my feelings.

Joanne – Thank you for "grounding me" and "lifting me up"!

Judith Kathleen Ji – You have helped me get on the plane to India so many times. I love and appreciate you! Thank you for always knowing when my tank was low…

Gur Ma Carolyn – American Holy Woman
Thank you for continuing to teach me to weigh all my actions against Eternity!

Yvonne Marie Larsen-Moorman – You had the premonition I was meant to help people with my intuition. Thank you!

Lorraine – Thank you for being my Angel.

Maggie LeDuc – Thank you for helping us "get outta Dodge!"

Sai Rita Ji - Thank you for your beautiful Baba heart.

Sister Mary Diane Scott - Head of "The God Squad." Angelic protector of tragically abandoned animals. Thank you!

Judy La Judy - Oil painting indeed! Thank you!!!

Georgina! Seva Queen! Lights, Camera, Reading Tour!!! Thank you!

Steve and Linda Smith - My heartfelt thanks for manifesting our precious home. May God Bless You!

My Theus Family - Londale, Martha, Kamaal and Londale Jr. Thank you for believing in Marc and I. Londale - "The Cop That Can Act." Londale, my Space Brother, you are bigger than life itself. Thank you for "reading" me. Martha - Crystal Clear Visionary of the movie industry. Thank you for keeping us _moving_ at all times. Kamaal - Angel, Supermodel, Artist, Actress. Thank you, for my cosmic book cover. Your love, intuition and purity shine through brilliantly!!! Londale Jr. - Actor/Comedian/Philanthropist. You're for doing it! You are breaking ground for all of us - pulling us forward.

My worldwide clients of many, many years. This book would not exist without you. You are the heroes in these tales. I love you all and thank you for trusting this frail, all-too-human psychic (a little).

Kathleen

Kathleen DuQuette
c/o Marc DuQuette
P.O. BOX 1313
Dripping Springs, TX 78620-1313
Email: Marc@MarcDuQuette.net

For all press and publicity, including radio interviews, please contact:
Martha Theus, 1st House Publishing
(424) 249-9355
Email: MarthaTheus@gmail.com

www.KathleenDuQuette.com